CW00767777

The Maximus Mouse
Primary Assembly Book

Brian Ogden

Illustrations by Elke Counsell

Scripture Union

The Maximus Mouse books:
Maximus Mouse
Maximus Rides Again
Maximus and the Great Expedition
Maximus and the Computer Mouse
Tales of Young Maximus
Maximus Mouse and Friends
The Adventures of Maximus Mouse
Maximus Mouse's Christmas Card

Other books by the same author:
Short Tails and Tall Stories
Aunt Emily's African Animals
Ryan the Lion

© Brian Ogden 2001

First published 2001

Scripture Union, 207–209 Queensway, Bletchley,
Milton Keynes, MK2 2EB, England.

ISBN 1 85999 492 X

British Library Cataloguing-in-Publication Data.
A catalogue record of this book is available from the British
Library.

Printed and bound in Malta by Interprint Ltd.

CONTENTS

INTRODUCTION

Maximus Mouse first scampered out of the vestry into St Michael's Church ten years ago. Since then his adventures have been recorded in more than ten books which have been widely used in Primary Schools. This book is a collection of some of the more popular stories presented in Assembly format.

Maximus has a number of friends: two other mice, Patrick and Paula, who live with their mouselings in the Sunday School cupboard, Barnabas the church bat, Harold, Herbert and various other hedgehogs, some rabbits, an owl called Mr Toot and Johann Sebastian, the organist's cat.

Many schools have found it helpful to have their own characters, especially Maximus. These can be made or bought and then produced when necessary. A small knitted mouse is ideal for the purpose. The illustrations at the top of each Assembly outline give some idea of what Maximus looks like but for more detail see Elke Counsell's illustrations in the Maximus books.

CONTENTS

The twenty-three stories are divided into four sections. The first six illustrate parts of the Lord's Prayer. The next eleven follow general themes, which are relevant to daily happenings in school. There are three stories based on popular parables told by Jesus and the final section offers stories for the three major festivals of Christmas, harvest and Easter.

Each assembly has a **Theme** to help teachers to select a story relevant to a current issue in school. The theme is amplified in the **Aim**. Under **Preparation** suggestions are given to assist in the presentation of the stories. Leaders will enlarge on their presentation according to the circumstances.

The **Stories** are best told rather than read. This can be a little daunting but a story put into the leader's own words will always have greater impact than one that is read. At the end of each story there is a **Final Comment**. These are only suggestions and it is far better that the leader speak to local circumstances. A **Prayer** summing up the theme is also included. At the end of each assembly several **Hymns** are suggested from *The Complete Come and Praise*.

One further suggestion is to encourage the children to write their own stories based on the characters, thus providing further Assemblies for school or class use.

I would like to thank Jo Dobbs for her help in updating the stories and adding to the list of hymns.

Brian Ogden

THE LORD'S PRAYER

1 HAROLD HAS A SURPRISE

Theme: The holiness of God's name

Aim: To introduce the Lord's Prayer and teach about God's name

Preparation: The words of the Lord's Prayer available for an overhead projector, as a poster or for individual children

> **Our Father, who art in heaven,
> hallowed be thy name**

Story

As the year turns from autumn to winter, Maximus starts to collect paper hankies. During the week, when there are no services at St Michael's Church, it can get quite cold. Maximus likes to make a nice warm bed out of anything he can find. Hankies are best for this. He sticks two together and then stuffs them with screwed up pages from an old hymnbook. Humans call this a duvet but for

Maximus it serves two purposes, it keeps him warm and when he wakes up he can have breakfast of bed.

During Sunday services he scampers quietly about hoping that someone will drop a hanky on the floor. One Sunday, as the people were praying, Maximus spotted a large white hanky lying on the floor near the organ. He knew it was safest to run about during hymns as people couldn't hear him. While he waited for the prayer to end he started to listen to what was being said.

Being a well brought up mouse, Maximus put his front paws together. He knew that the people were talking to God and he heard them say 'Our Father, who art in heaven, Harold be thy name.'

He could not believe his furry ears – Harold the hedgehog was God! Surely not – he was only an ordinary hedgehog, nice enough, but not the God that the humans talked about in church. But they had said 'Harold be thy name' when they were talking to God. Then the vicar started speaking and Maximus, who had forgotten about the handkerchief when he heard about Harold, had to stay still and listen.

"The friends of Jesus," said the vicar, "once asked him to teach them to pray. 'When you pray,' replied Jesus, 'say our Father, who art in heaven, hallowed be thy name.'"

The vicar told all the people that they should think of God as a good father – one who loves us, cares about us, and always knows what is best for us. We should do what he tells us to do. But, if we do something which we know is wrong, he will still love us. If we are sorry then he will forgive us.

"This father," said the vicar, "lives in what we call heaven. That is a wonderful place where everyone is happy and no one is ill. It is the place where we go when we have finished here on earth if we love God.

"God's name is very special," the vicar went on, "it is a holy name. We should only use it when we are speaking to God. God's name is not something to say when things go wrong. God's name is ..."

"Wait for it," thought Maximus. "I know. His name is Harold."

"Is hallowed," said the vicar. "Hallowed means holy and precious."

"Oh dear," thought Maximus. "I've got it all wrong again. It isn't Harold after all."

That afternoon he went out into the churchyard and shared the joke with Harold. The little hedgehog thought it was very funny.

Final Comment: The use of appropriate language in school.

Prayer
Our Father,
Help us never to use your name wrongly but always to respect it and keep it holy. Amen

Hymn
51   Our Father
9   Fill your hearts with joy and gladness
63   Spirit of God
76   God in his love for us lent us this planet

2 UNCLE TOMOUSE'S WILL

Theme: Doing what is best

Aim: To help the children to understand that God's way is the best way

Preparation: The Lord's Prayer as before.
A letter addressed to Maximus

**Thy kingdom come; thy will be done;
on earth as it is in heaven**

Story

Maximus was dreaming in bed one morning when he was woken up by the sound of something being pushed through his letterbox. He struggled out of his hanky duvet and scampered over to the door. On the mat was a large white envelope. It looked like a very important letter.

Maximus didn't get many important letters. He

tore open the envelope and pulled out the important looking letter. It was from Foot, Foot, Foot and Mouth: Solicitors.

Dear Mr Maximus Mouse,

I regret to inform you that your Great Uncle Tomouse has died. Please come to these offices for the reading of his will next Monday at 10.00 a.m.

Yours faithfully,

A. Foot

On Monday morning Maximus was up early and soon found his way to Foot, Foot, Foot and Mouth: Solicitors. He was shown into a large room and was pleased to see lots of members of the family that he had not met for a long time. There were dozens of cousins, numbers of nephews, several sisters and bags of brothers. They all went silent when Mr Foot stood up to squeak.

"This is the last will and testament of Tomouse," he read. "I, Tomouse, being of sound mind do bequeath to all my nephews cheese for one year, in equal portions."

There were other gifts in Uncle Tomouse's will but Maximus didn't hear them. He was dreaming of all that lovely cheese – a whole year's supply. Good old Uncle Tomouse. He said goodbye to all his relations and went back home to the church.

The following Sunday Maximus was in church once again for the morning service. Last week he had learned that God was like a father and that his name was holy. He wondered what he would hear today.

"Thy kingdom come, thy will be done, on earth as it is in heaven," announced the vicar.

"Bless my tail and whiskers," said Maximus. "The vicar is going to read a will. Perhaps we shall all get something."

"The kingdom of God can only come when we all do the will of God," said the vicar. "To do the will of God is to do what he wants; to love him and to love everybody we know. We should be kind and thoughtful and think of other people before we think about ourselves. That is the will of God. Those who have finished their lives here on earth go to heaven if they love God. In heaven everyone does what God wants because they love him. On earth we have to try every day to do his will. Then we help God to make the kingdom of earth more like the kingdom of heaven."

Maximus scratched his head with his front paws and thought about what the vicar had said. He scuttled away as the people sang the last hymn. Then he remembered the cheese he had been left in his uncle's will and made a delicious cheese sandwich for lunch.

Final Comment: We really should think carefully about it when we say 'thy will be done.'

Prayer

Heavenly Father,
We know that what you want us to do is best for
our lives. Help us to know your will and give us the
courage to do it. Amen

Hymn

44   He who would valiant be
51   Our Father
5   Carpenter, carpenter, make me a tree
30   Thank him for the town and country
38   Now thank we all our God
43   Give me oil in my lamp

3 CANDLEWAX AND CHEESE PIE

Theme: Everyone needs daily bread

Aim: To show that we can all help people in need

Preparation: The Lord's Prayer as before
A display of the work of any charity supported by the school or a reminder of it.

Give us this day our daily bread

Story

Maximus was having an afternoon nap. He was curled up, near the back of the church, in a pool of sunshine which was streaming in through the window.

He had been very busy that morning making a new duvet from a nice hanky that the organist had dropped at choir practice. He had to make a new one as he had eaten the old one when he woke up hungry in the night. Just as he was dreaming of candlewax and cheese pie there was a loud noise. The noise came from the back of the church. Maximus jumped up, rubbed his eyes, and scampered under a chair.

Several people had come into the back of the church. They were carrying large pieces of card and strips of metal. Maximus watched as they slotted the strips together and put the large cards on them. After a while the people went away and Maximus ran down the church to see what this strange looking thing was. On the cards were some large photographs. They showed some people in another country. The people seemed to be very hungry and their clothes were not much more than rags.

Another photograph showed children holding a bowl. Maximus read the words printed on the bottom – GIVE US THIS DAY OUR DAILY BREAD. He stroked his whiskers with his front paws. He had heard the vicar talking about helping others and how the church tried to give money and pray for those who were starving. Maximus had never seen a photograph of hungry children before and he felt very sorry for them.

Just as he was thinking how dreadful it must be to be so hungry he heard a strange noise coming from the vestry. As he arrived at the door he saw the front half of another mouse coming through his hole in the wall.

"Stay right there!" shouted Maximus, sounding much braver than he felt. "What do you think you're doing coming into my church?"

"Please," begged the other mouse, "please let me come in."

"All right," said Maximus. "Come in, but no funny tricks."

The strange mouse pulled himself through the hole and dropped down onto the floor.

"Is that candlewax and cheese pie I can smell?" he asked.

Maximus saw how cold and wet and hungry he looked. Instead of being frightened of this stranger he began to feel very sorry for him. Maximus discovered that his new friend was called Patrick. Patrick had been living in an old house down the road. An elderly lady owned it but she had gone into a special home when she could no longer look after herself. The council had come along and knocked down her house to build a new road. Patrick and his family had nowhere to live. They had lost all their clothes and furniture and food.

"I left my wife and mouselings under a hedge," said Patrick, "because it was raining so hard. I promised I would find them something to eat and a new home."

Maximus warmed up some of the candlewax and cheese pie. Patrick ate it noisily and soon finished off a very large portion.

"I think the best thing to do," suggested Maximus, "would be to move you all into the church. Let me show you."

Patrick had never been in a church before. It was very big, but then his family was growing.

"This is the Sunday School cupboard," said

Maximus. "I think you could all be very comfortable in here."

"There are lots of things for the mouselings to do as well," said Patrick. "Paper for them to draw on, books to read, and wax crayons to eat."

Patrick went back through the hole in the vestry wall. Soon all the family was safely settled in the cupboard.

The next day was Sunday. Maximus was pleased to see that Patrick, his wife Paula, and the mouselings were all in church for the service.

"Give us this day our daily bread," said the vicar. "Most of us don't have to think about our daily bread. We take it for granted that we will have more than enough to eat. At the end of the day we expect to go to bed full and not hungry. In many parts of the world these words are really a prayer asking God for the food the people need to live. It is our duty as Christians to care about those who do not have enough to eat. We must do everything we can to help. Some of us can give money. All of us can pray. Sometimes we can care for those who live near us by making friends with them and doing practical things to help."

It was all Maximus could do to stay quiet. He wanted to tell the vicar about how he had helped Patrick and his family. Just in time he remembered to whisper it to himself. He cooked a very special meal that evening of hymnbook hotpot. Then he invited them all to supper.

Final Comment: Remind the children of their support for the school charity.

Prayer

Father God,
Thank you for all the good things you give us: our health, our homes, our food and our friends. We are sorry that so often we take them all for granted. Help us to understand what it is to need these things and give us the love to provide them for others. Amen

Hymn

94   Make us worthy Lord
139 Now the harvest is all gathered in
30   Thank him for the town and country
31   Can you be sure that the rain will fall?
32   Thank you, Lord, for this new day
36   God is love: his the care
40   Praise him, praise him
43   Give me oil in my lamp, keep me burning

4 DIS-ORGAN-ISED

Theme: Forgiving and forgiven

Aim: To show that to be forgiven we must be sorry

Preparation: The Lord's Prayer as before
Organ music as the children enter
and leave the assembly

> **And forgive us our trespasses,
> as we forgive them that trespass against us**

Story

Maximus loves music. He could sit and eat it for hours. Sometimes he fries it, sometimes he bakes it and sometimes he just eats it raw. He also liked to listen to music. Maximus likes to sit and listen when the organist comes in to practise the hymns for the coming Sunday. Sometimes Maximus joins in on his mouseorgan.

The organ in the church was very old. From time to time it made very strange noises in the middle of hymns. A special organ repairman came to look at it. After he had checked it out and listened once or twice he spoke to the organist and the vicar.

"I'm sorry but there is nothing I can do. It is just too old to repair. You will have to buy a new one."

Several months later the new organ was brought into the church and fitted carefully in place. The organist played some hymns and he and the vicar agreed that it sounded much better than the old one. There were no strange noises any more. The organist was really looking forward to playing the new organ at the church services.

The next night Maximus decided to explore the new organ. He could see quite well because the moon shone in through the church windows.

Maximus climbed the north face of the keyboard and soon found a mouse-sized hole. Inside, the organ was very different from the old one. Everything was electronic. There were hundreds of brightly covered wires. Maximus scampered all over it – sliding down one wire, nibbling through another one, and even swapping some over. It was much more exciting than the old organ. He enjoyed himself so much that he couldn't wait to come again another night. He scampered back to the vestry and was soon fast asleep.

Just as Maximus was dreaming about showing Patrick and the mouselings round the new organ, he was woken by the sound of voices. The vicar and the choirboys came into the vestry to get ready for the morning service. Maximus heard them talking about the new organ and how good it would be singing to it. Maximus followed them all into church. The vicar announced the first hymn. The organist put his fingers on the keys.

There was the most *DREADFUL* noise. It was nothing at all like a hymn tune. It was then that Maximus realised what he had done. He had changed the wires around so much inside the organ that it could not be used.

Back in the vestry after the service, which had been rather spoiled without the new organ, Maximus decided to go back to bed again. After all he had been up all night. He went over to the corner where he kept his little duvet. *IT WASN'T THERE.* He searched everywhere for it. He looked in the cupboards, under the carpet, even in the waste bin, but he couldn't see it anywhere.

"I'll go and ask Patrick if he knows where it is," said Maximus to himself.

As he reached the Sunday School cupboard he saw Patrick unrolling a duvet.

"That's mine!" shouted Maximus. "You've stolen my duvet."

"I didn't think you'd mind," said Patrick. "You see, Paula is not very well. I need it to keep her warm."

"Well, you might have asked, but since you need it I will forgive you. Just ask if you want anything."

On Monday, a repairman came from the organ firm.

"Looks like something small and furry's been in here," said the repairman.

The next Sunday morning the vicar continued his talks about the Lord's Prayer.

"Forgive us our trespasses as we forgive them that trespass against us," he said. "Trespass is an old word meaning sin or the things that we do that are wrong. For example, last Sunday, we had a problem with our new organ. It seems that someone small, like our church mouse, got inside it and re-arranged the wires. That was a wrong thing to do and it has caused us a lot of trouble. But we forgive him for doing this, providing he never does it again."

Maximus was very ashamed at hearing this. He was really sorry for what he had done. Then he thought about Patrick and the duvet. He was glad he had forgiven Patrick for taking it but he was even happier that he had been forgiven for spoiling the new organ. He sat and enjoyed listening to the organ. This time everyone joined in the hymns without any funny noises.

Final Comment: To be forgiven we must learn to forgive.

Prayer

Heavenly Father,
We so often ask you for forgiveness but we are not good at forgiving those that hurt us. Help us to forgive others and to know that you will always forgive us when we are really sorry. Amen

Hymn

25   When Jesus walked in Galilee
51   Our Father
85   Spirit of peace, come to our waiting world
87   Give me hope, Lord, for each day

5   HIDDEN SECRETS

Theme: Making choices

Aim: To think about the issue of temptation

Preparation: The Lord's Prayer as before
A box with FUDGE printed on it

**And lead us not into temptation:
but deliver us from evil**

Story

You may have guessed by now that Maximus is a rather greedy mouse. You have heard quite a lot about what he eats. Candlewax and cheese sandwiches, wax waffles and music muesli are all favourite items on his menu.

But Maximus is not the only one who likes his food. I have to tell you that the vicar of St Michael's Church is also very fond of certain things to eat.

Mrs Vicar gets very cross with the vicar and tells him that he must lose weight or he will not get into his cassock. The cassock is the long black sort of dressing gown which vicars wear so that people can't see their knees knocking when they are nervous.

Mrs Vicar had told her husband that he must not eat any more sweets. The vicar loved sweets but his special treat was fudge. He adored fudge: fudge with nuts, fudge with ginger, fudge with rum and raisins, chocolate fudge, in fact any sort of fudge.

One Christmas, the church organist, who knew how much the vicar liked it, gave him a large box of nut and ginger fudge. The vicar was afraid that Mrs Vicar would find it and give it to the choirboys. Instead of taking it home he put it in the drawer in the vestry where he kept all his special things. Sometimes, before a service, the vicar would secretly take out a piece of fudge and chew it when he thought no one was watching.

One Sunday morning Maximus was snuggled down in his duvet wondering if the music of 'Fight the good fight', which he had eaten for breakfast, would give him tummy ache. He happened to look up just as the vicar took a bite of ginger fudge. Maximus made a note to remember what he had seen and went back to sleep again.

Later that morning, after all the choirboys and the vicar had gone home, Maximus searched the drawers for the fudge. Mice are very good at finding food that has a strong smell. He knew exactly where he would find it. He pushed aside two old hymnbooks, a stack of out of date notices and one half of a pair of red woolly gloves that had been left in church. The end of the box was open and Maximus took a mouse-watering bite of ginger fudge.

Just as he was thinking of moving onto a slice of nut fudge the door burst open and in came the vicar. He had forgotten his diary. Fortunately he didn't see Maximus who was lying very still pretending to be a furry glove. Maximus was so frightened that as soon as the vicar left he jumped down out of the drawer. He ran, as fast as his little paws could manage, to hide under the old carpet in the corner. He decided against eating any more fudge for lunch and was very glad not to have been caught.

The following Sunday morning the vicar told the people that he had come to the words 'lead us not into temptation but deliver us from evil,' in the Lord's Prayer.

" 'Lead us not into temptation' is an asking prayer," he said. "We are asking God that we are not tempted to do something wrong. Sometimes we want to do things, which we know are wrong – this wanting is what we call temptation. We are asking God to help us not to give in to this wanting.

" 'Deliver us from evil' is also an asking prayer. We ask God to stop anything bad from happening to us. These two parts of the Lord's Prayer are prayers for ourselves – that we don't do wrong things and that wrong things don't happen to us."

Maximus, who had been listening, suddenly thought of what had happened last Sunday morning. He had been tempted to eat the vicar's fudge and had nearly been caught doing so.

"I think that prayer is the right one for me," said Maximus to himself. "Lead me not into temptation but deliver me from evil. I must leave the fudge for the vicar, but I hope Mrs Vicar doesn't find out!"

Final Comment: We have to make choices many times each day. Sometimes we need to think about them carefully.

Prayer
Father God,
Help us to know what is wrong and to do what is right so that we may be true friends of yours. Amen

Hymn
23   Jesus good above all other
51   Our Father
87   Give us hope, Lord, for each day
89   Guess how I feel
103   The road of life lies before me

6   TOP OF THE FORM

Theme: A great God

Aim: to learn about the greatness of God

Preparation: The Lord's Prayer as before
A brown envelope

> **For thine is the kingdom, the power and
> the glory, forever and ever. Amen**

Story

Maximus hated official looking forms. They always gave him a headache. Every now and then the postmouse would deliver another brown envelope. Maximus always sat and looked at them and hoped they would go away. Sooner or later, though, he had to fill them in and it always took him ages.

One morning, as Maximus was lying in bed, he heard a letter flop onto the floor of the vestry. He fought his way out of his duvet and then groaned when he saw the colour of the envelope. It was light brown. Maximus knew light brown envelopes always had forms in them.

"It's not going to be a good day," moaned Maximus to the vestry wall. "In fact, it's going to be a really boring day. I *hate* forms."

Maximus threw the brown envelope down on the floor and went off to find some breakfast. He banged the vestry door behind him and scampered around the church hoping to find a nice piece of music to eat. After a long search he found an old hymnbook near the organ and helped himself to numbers 475 to 483. There was no sign of Patrick in the church so Maximus went over to the Sunday School cupboard to find him. When he opened the cupboard door he could see that Patrick was writing.

"Sorry, I can't come out just at the moment," said Patrick. "I've got this census form to fill in."

"Oh, I had one of those horrid things," said Maximus. "I'm not going to waste my time filling it in."

"But you've got to," replied Patrick, "it's come from the Mouse of Commons. Every mouse must fill one in and send it back. They need to know all about you. Tell you what. If you like, when I've finished mine, I'll come and help you."

Later that morning Patrick explained to Maximus that every few years every mouse in the country had to fill in a census form. The Mouse of Commons needed to know all about everyone – when they were born, where they lived, what work they did, and lots more. Between them they soon managed to answer all the questions on the form.

"Now they will know as much about me as I know about myself," said Maximus.

The two friends folded up the forms and took them to the post box. Maximus felt very pleased that he had got the job finished and thanked Patrick for his help.

The following Sunday morning Maximus was up early. He was anxious not to miss the vicar's talk. It was the last one about the Lord's Prayer. He found a warm place near one of the radiators, he joined in the hymns, and settled down to listen to the vicar.

"We have come to the last part of the Lord's Prayer today," he said. "'For thine is the kingdom, the power and the glory, forever and ever. Amen.' At the beginning of this prayer we learned about God being our father. At the end we learn even more about him. The kingdom that matters is God's kingdom in which everyone does what God wants. God is all-powerful – he made us and he made the world. He is wonderful and we praise and thank him for what he is when we say he is glorious. God is so much greater than we can imagine.

"There has never been a time without God and there never will be – he is forever and ever. And then finally we say Amen. Amen means 'so be it'. Whenever we use the word 'Amen' we are saying we agree with whatever the prayer says."

Maximus thought about the census form that he had filled in.

"It's a bit like that. I've written down a lot about myself so someone now knows a lot about me. Jesus gave his friends the Lord's Prayer to use and now we know a lot more about God. I must go and tell Patrick all about it."

Final Comment: God is greater than anything or anyone we know.

Prayer
Father God,
You are greater than we can possibly understand yet your love for us is that of a father for his children. Help us to show, by the way we live, that we are members of your kingdom here on earth. Amen

Hymn
36   God is love, his the care
133 Praise the Lord
15   There are hundreds of sparrows
16   When God made the garden of creation
17   Think of a world without any flowers
18   He gave me eyes so I could see
19   He's got the whole world in his hand

GENERAL THEMES

7 REAL MICE ARE GREY

Theme: We're all different

Aim: To show that it is what we are that counts – not what we look like.

Preparation: Some holiday brochures to hold up.

Story

"The trouble with foreigners," said Maximus to Patrick, "is that they squeak foreign."

The two mice had been discussing holidays. Maximus had never been abroad for his holidays. He stayed with various friends and family from time to time, but unlike Patrick and his family, had never left England.

"Of course they do," laughed Patrick. "To them you squeak foreign too! Just because a mouse doesn't squeak the same language as you, or eat the same food..."

"Yes, that's another thing," interrupted Maximus. "All that horrible smelly cheese – blue with little worms crawling in and out of it. Or what's that other one – all full of holes. Why pay for cheese with holes in it? It only goes to show what foreign mice are like."

"Maximus, you are so wrong," argued Patrick. "If only you would go and see for yourself. We had a really fantastic holiday last year in Miceland. The weather was hot, the food was good, and most of all the mice were really friendly. Most of them squeak English. Just as well, since so few English mice squeak any foreign languages at all."

"No, it's just not right," said Maximus. "As far as I'm concerned we grey mice are different from those foreign white mice. They should all learn to squeak proper English and eat decent food. We should keep ourselves to ourselves. All those foreign mice are coming over here and taking our jobs. I expect if you went to some of our churches you would find a white mouse as mouse-keeper. Those white mice are getting everywhere."

"But they're exactly the same as us!" exploded Patrick. "They may be a different colour and squeak another language but they are the same as you and me."

"Sorry, Patrick, but I think you're wrong," said Maximus. And he turned away from his friend and scampered off to look for some lunch. He muttered to himself as he went. "White mice indeed – it's just not natural. Proper mice are grey – not white."

It was not the first time that Maximus and Patrick had argued over grey and white mice. Patrick had tried hard to make Maximus understand that white mice were the same as grey mice. But Maximus's mind was made up and he wouldn't listen to anyone else.

Just as Patrick was going back to have lunch with his family in the Sunday School cupboard he heard a loud bang. This was followed by a shout. Patrick scampered, as fast as his paws could manage, towards the noise. By the pulpit he saw something very odd. There was a large book lying on the ground. The book was moving slowly up and down. Every time it went down a groan came from underneath it.

Patrick, rather nervously, went up to the book. He lifted one corner as it rose in the air. Underneath he saw a very unhappy looking Maximus.

"Get this off me," moaned Maximus. "I think I've broken my leg!"

"Whatever happened?" asked Patrick as he gently lifted the book.

"I climbed the pulpit to get the vicar's sermon notes for lunch. Fresh sermon notes are really good for you. But I overbalanced on the top and fell down. Then the vicar's hymnbook fell on top of me. I've been mugged by a hymnbook!"

Patrick took a close look at his friend. Maximus' leg was beginning to go a very strange colour.

"I'm going to phone for the doctor. He'll decide what to do about your leg. I'm afraid that you may have to go to hospital."

A quarter of an hour later the church door opened and in came a mouse carrying a big black bag. Patrick, who had been waiting at the back of the church, gave a loud gasp. The doctor was a white mouse. Their usual doctor was a grey mouse like them. Patrick took him to Maximus.

"Now what seems to be the trouble?" asked the doctor in perfect English. "It's Mr Maximus, isn't it?"

"Yes," stuttered Maximus, looking at the doctor. "I fell from the pulpit and I think I've broken my leg."

The doctor felt his leg very gently. He asked Maximus to bend it and then to wiggle it about.

"No," said the doctor with a smile. "You have been very lucky this time. It is badly bruised and you will have to rest it for several days – but it isn't broken. Now perhaps between us we can get you to bed."

Patrick stayed with Maximus after the doctor had left. He looked at Maximus with a smile.

"There you are," he said, "you are a real fraud. You didn't mind a white mouse doctor helping you when you needed it, did you?"

"No, you're right Patrick. He was very kind. I expect all white mice are really like that – just the same as us."

And Maximus thought a lot more about it as his leg got better.

Final Comment: We need to get to know people before we make up our minds about them.

Prayer

Heavenly Father,
We often think wrong things about people we don't
really know. Forgive us and help us to understand
that we can learn a great deal from each other.
Amen

Hymn

67   The ink is black
69   I belong to a family
70   Would you walk by on the other side
65   When I needed a neighbour

8 BATMAN AND PATRICK THE MOUSE WONDER

Theme: Bad temper

Aim: To show that being bad tempered can spoil friendships

Preparation: Picture or soft toy of a bat

Story

It was not a good day for Maximus. First of all, he had not slept very well. He had found an old hymnbook behind the organ which must have been there for years. He had seven hymns for supper and then had tummy ache all night. But there had been another problem as well. For the past few nights he had been nibbling away at his paper hanky duvet. This meant holes. And where there are holes there are paws to fill them. He had woken up with very cold feet.

Maximus was expecting a letter from his cousin Chrismus. He was hoping to stay with Chrismus for a short holiday but no invitation had arrived. Maximus was still feeling rather ill from the seven hymns and he didn't want any breakfast. The truth was that Maximus was very cross with the world.

"I'm fed up, fed up, fed up!" he shouted as he stumped down the aisle of the church. "Nobody cares about me. Nobody cares that I've got tummy ache," he grumbled. "I spend all my time looking after the church, but does anyone look after me? No, of course they don't. I might as well go and find a proper mousehole of my own."

At that moment Barnabas, the church bat who lives in the belfry, came swooping down. He was flapping his wings and causing quite a wind.

"Go away, you beastly bat," shouted Maximus. "Can't you see I've got tummy ache? All you bats do is frighten respectable mice by your low flying. Don't you know there is a law against low flying bats in churches?"

"A rodent with resentment, a moody mouse," said Barnabas. "A creature without composure."

Patrick heard all the noise going on in the church and scampered out to see what was happening. He skidded on the newly polished church floor and crashed straight into Maximus.

"Can't you mind out where you're going?" shouted Maximus angrily. "Here I am minding my own tummy ache, not disturbing anyone. First I'm attacked by a dive-bombing bat and then by a crazy mouse that thinks he's a Formula One driver. I thought that churches were supposed to be places of peace and quiet. Fat chance of finding any here with you two about."

Maximus turned round and tried to look very fierce as he walked slowly back to the vestry. He could hear Barnabas and Patrick talking to each other.

"Our mutual friend appears to be irrationally irritated," said Barnabas. "He is in an unhappy humour."

"Yes, I think we'll have to do something to cheer him up," said Patrick. "I've got an idea."

The mouse and the bat went to the back of the church and whispered to each other. Moments later Barnabas flew back to the belfry and Patrick disappeared into the Sunday School cupboard.

Maximus, who had fallen asleep in the vestry, was woken by a loud knocking on the door. He tumbled out of bed and grumpily opened the door.

"What is it now?" he started to say, and then stopped in surprise. Standing at the door were two of the strangest looking beings he had ever seen. Barnabas's face was covered with a mask and a cloak hung over his wings. Patrick was dressed in a cloak made from an old tissue and also wore a mask.

"Enter Batman and Patrick the Mouse Wonder!" said Barnabas.

"We've come to cheer you up," said Patrick. "We fight all the things that make mice bad tempered!"

By this time Maximus was laughing so much he couldn't squeak. They both looked so funny.

Barnabas' wings were sticking through his cloak and Patrick's whiskers were caught in his mask making him sneeze. Maximus lay down on the floor and laughed and laughed and laughed.

Later, after a special tea party, Maximus thanked his two friends for making him happy again. He told them he was sorry for being such a bad tempered mouse.

Final Comment: Being bad tempered can spoil lots of things. It's good to have friends who help to change our moods.

Prayer
Loving Father,
Forgive us when we are bad tempered and selfish.
Help us to remember how much you have given us
and to be thankful. Amen

Hymn
141 Shalom, Shalom
147 Make me a channel of your peace
144 Peace is flowing like a river

9 READ THE RULES

Theme: Keeping rules

Aim: To show the importance of keeping rules

Preparation: A list of agreed classroom rules

Story

"For goodness sake, Maximus, slow down!" shouted Patrick. "You'll have a terrible accident. STOP! MAXIMUS, STOP!"

The two mice, Maximus and Patrick, were out in the churchyard. They had saved up to buy a skateboard. It was ten centimetres long and they had painted it luminous green. They found an old piece of fence and leant it against a gravestone to make a ramp. Maximus climbed the ramp, jumped onto the skateboard and, with a shout of "Geronimouse!", hurtled down the ramp. He landed on his nose in the soft grass.

"OUCH! In fact, double ouch," cried Maximus, rubbing his nose. "That hurt. But did you see me go? Must have been faster than Tom chasing Jerry."

"I really think that we should read the booklet," suggested Patrick. "It said on the box, 'Read Rules before Starting'. Here we are, now what do they say?"

And this is what Patrick read:

1   *Never skateboard without a hard hat.*
2   *Always wear pads on your knees and elbows.*
3   *Make sure you know where you will land if you jump.*
4   *Do not skateboard where there are other animals.*

"You're a spoilsport," said Maximus. "We're only just trying it out. Patrick, are you going to have your go?"

"Not until we've got the right gear," said Patrick. "Let's go and sort out what we need."

The two friends carried the board between them back into the church. They put it down in the vestry and began to make kneepads from a piece of grubby paper handkerchief.

"What are we going to do about crash helmets?" asked Maximus.

"I've had an idea about them," said Patrick. "Do you remember those walnuts we had the other day? I reckon the shells would make perfect crash hats."

"Brilliant! Can't wait to try one on. Come on, let's go and get them."

The two mice scampered out of the vestry and ran round to the dustbin. They scrambled up the side and started to search for the walnut shells. After looking through some very smelly old flowers, some very soggy teabags and some old service sheets they found what they were looking for – two shells. They scooped out the middle bits and tried them on.

"Fantastic! Couldn't be better," said Patrick. "Quick. Get out. I can hear the dustmen coming."

Just in time the two mice jumped to the ground clutching their shells and scurried back to the church.

"Well," said Patrick, "I must get back to Paula and the mouselings – it's supper time. See you in the morning."

Maximus went back to the vestry and looked at the gleaming skateboard. He walked all the way round it, admiring the bright paint, the shining silver coloured wheels, the names they had painted on the side – Mighty Max and Powerful Pat.

"Be a pity not to try it again," said Maximus out loud. "It'll be safe enough in the church."

He put all four paws firmly on the ground and pushed as hard as he could with his shoulder. The skateboard moved slowly out of the vestry and into the church. Maximus needed a slope to give him speed and the two steps down into the nave of the church were just right for that.

Maximus stepped onto the skateboard and gave a big push with one paw on the ground. The board began to move faster and faster. He just managed to keep his balance as the board bounced down the steps into the aisle. By this time the skateboard was going so fast it was all that Maximus could do to hang on with all four paws.

In the distance Maximus could see the font which stood in the middle of the aisle at the end of the church. It got bigger and bigger as Maximus got nearer and nearer. By this time he was yelling at the top of his squeak.

"HELP! PLEASE SOME MOUSE HELP ME!"

At the same moment that Maximus crashed into the font Patrick came rushing out of the Sunday School cupboard.

"Maximus, what are you doing? Are you all right? What's more important, is the skateboard all right?"

Maximus lay at the foot of the font moaning loudly and holding his head with his paws. When Patrick reached him Maximus opened one eye, and looked up.

"I've broken my head," he said. "I'm sure it's split in two ... oh, oh, oh."

"And where, may I ask, is your crash nut?" demanded Patrick. "You deserve a broken head for not wearing it. Mice that break rules get into trouble."

The next morning Maximus woke up with a terrible headache. He felt bruised all over and had a very black eye. When Patrick came to see him, Maximus was a very quiet and sorry-for-himself mouse.

"I'm really sorry," he said. "I promise to keep the rules in future – I will wear my crash nut and the protectors."

Patrick forgave his friend and they repainted the skateboard where it had been scratched. They had lots of fun on it but always kept the rules and didn't get hurt any more.

Final Comment: Rules are made to make life better for everyone.

Prayer
Heavenly Father,
You have given us rules to live by which are meant to keep us safe. Help us to keep them. Most of all, may we love you and love our friends. Amen

Hymn
103   The road of life lies before me
113   A time to be born
42   Travel on, travel on, there's a river that is flowing
45   The journey of life

10 | A GAME OF FOOTSNAIL

Theme: Bullying

Aim: To consider the problem of bullying

Preparation: A popular football club shirt

Story

"Stop it, please stop it," begged the snail. "I'm getting dizzy. You're hurting me. Please stop."

But Maximus and Patrick took no notice of the little creature and carried on kicking it.

"It's my turn in goal," said Maximus. "You've been in for ages."

The two mice swapped over. The goal posts were two hymnbooks standing on the church floor. The two mice were wearing their teams' kit – Maximus supported Mousehampton United and Patrick was a fan of Mousenal.

Patrick dribbled the snail round a flower stand and took a mighty kick. The poor snail shot straight over Maximus's head and landed with a crash against the wall.

"That's your worst shot yet," laughed Maximus. "Thought we were playing pawball not basketball!"

The snail pushed his head out of his shell. He shook it from side to side to make sure his neck was still working. Then he began to slide away as quietly and quickly as possible.

"I don't think our creepy friend wants to play any more," said Patrick. "I don't think he likes pawball."

"Oh let him go," said Maximus. "Some creatures are just not born to be great pawballers like me. It's time we had a rest. Let's see what we can find to eat."

The two mice had been playing pawball in church using the snail as their ball. They walked out of the church into the bright sunshine, chatting about the game.

"Fantastic shot that last one of yours," said Maximus. "It went so high I bet the snail wished he had a parachute!"

"You're not much better," said his friend. "You kicked him into the flower vase and he nearly drowned."

The mice wandered around between the gravestones, kicking pebbles to each other and boasting about their pawball skills. They did not notice the large white eyes looking down from the church tower, nor the grey black feathers ruffling in the breeze.

With barely a sound, Jack and Doris, the two jackdaws that nest in the tower, swooped down and snatched the mice in their feet. Before either Maximus or Patrick could say 'Cheddar cheese' they were off the ground hanging beneath the two birds.

The mice were terrified. One minute they had been happily kicking about in the churchyard, the next they were flying high above the church held tightly by the claws of the jackdaws. Maximus and Patrick were squeakless. There was nothing they could do. They were held very tight by the claws of the birds. If they wriggled loose they would fall to the ground – a long way below them.

"Help! Help!" squeaked Maximus at last getting his squeak back. "You're hurting me. Please stop. Please put us down."

"Now where have I heard that before?" asked John as he flew round the churchyard in a large circle.

"Well, dear," replied his wife, only a wing tip away, "I seem to remember hearing it in the church not very long ago. I think it was a poor frightened snail who was asking for help."

"And I remember seeing two macho mice bravely kicking a snail about," said her partner.

"I think we had better land and talk about all this," said Doris.

The two birds, with their cargoes of very scared mice, landed on the ledge of the tower. They put the mice down unhurt on the ledge. Maximus immediately put his paws over his eyes.

"I think I'm going to be sick," he whimpered. "I can't stand heights. I get frightened on a thick pile carpet."

It was Patrick who came to his senses, although he was shaking with fear.

"Please sir," he said looking at John Jackdaw, "what are you going to do with us?"

"We haven't quite decided yet," said the jackdaw, fluttering his wings to stay on the draughty ledge. "You do understand that we jackdaws rather fancy a meal of mice. My wife has lots of mice recipes."

Yes," said Doris, "John likes fried mice and I'm very fond of mice pudding!"

"But ... but we're church mice; we never do anybody any harm."

"That's not what we saw and heard," said Doris. "You were being very cruel to the snail. You kicked him all over the church and laughed when he begged you to stop."

"We're really sorry," said Patrick.

"We'll never do it again," said Maximus.

"We didn't mean to hurt him," added Patrick. "I hope he's all right."

"Well, on this occasion we might just let you go," said John. "But let this be a warning to you. Never bully creatures smaller than yourselves. You don't like being frightened and neither do they."

Once more the jackdaws held the two mice tight in their claws. The birds took off from the tower ledge and landed gracefully back in the churchyard. Maximus and Patrick shook themselves, glad to be free, and scampered into the church having learnt a lesson.

Final Comment: Many children and adults are bullied. It is never right to bully others but we can help those who have been bullied.

Prayer
Loving Father,
We pray for all those children and adults in the world who are bullied by others. Help us to support them by our friendship. Give us the courage to challenge those who are bullies. Amen

Hymn
65   When I needed a neighbour were you there?
71   If I had a hammer
79   From the tiny ant
94   Make us worthy, Lord

11 MAXIMUS SAYS NO!

Theme: Selfishness

Aim: To show that we should consider other people before we think about ourselves

Preparation: Poster showing Willy and the Whisker Bangers

Story

"I'm sure that Maximus will do it," said Paula. "He never minds looking after the mouselings when we go out. Why don't you go and ask him now?"

"Right," said Patrick, "I'll see if he will. I'm really looking forward to the music – it's not often that Willy and the Whisker Bangers get to play gigs round here."

Patrick scampered off to the vestry where he found Maximus struggling to get up from his duvet.

"Maximus, old friend, Paula and I wondered if you would do us a favour tonight? You see we've got tickets for Willy and the Whisker Bangers and we need a mouseling sitter. Any chance you can help?"

"Not tonight," said Maximus, "no, not tonight. You see it's my favourite telly tonight – it's *Coronation Mouseholes*. I never miss that. Sorry, but you'll have to find someone else."

Patrick went back to Paula a very disappointed mouse. Meanwhile Maximus got washed and dressed. Then he went out into the church to look for some breakfast. It had been choir practice the night before and sometimes one of the choirboys dropped a sweet. Just as he found a rather grubby piece of chocolate he heard a strange sound. It felt like a draught, as though the window had been opened on a windy day. Then he heard flapping wings and realised it was Barnabas the church bat.

"I say, you – er, Minibus, or whatever your name is," said the bat, "could you do me a favour? I've got a hospital appointment – got to have my batteries charged. I'm expecting a parcel in the post this afternoon. It's a special book called *The Bats of Britain* – all about bats in the war. Would you mind taking it in for me?"

"No, not this afternoon," said Maximus, "no way, it can't be done. I'm off skateboarding this afternoon. Got to get fit you know. You'll have to ask someone else for your parcel."

Barnabas flew off feeling very disappointed. Maximus went back to the chocolate. As it was a beautiful day Maximus took it into the churchyard. He sat down on a gravestone to finish his breakfast.

Just as he was brushing away the bits of chocolate that had fallen in his fur he heard a rustling sound in the grass. A snout followed by two eyes followed by what looked like a pincushion came out of the grass. It was Herbert the hedgehog.

"Ah, Maximus, just the mouse I was hoping to see," said Herbert. "You remember my daughter Henrietta, whom you saved from drowning in the pond? Well, she's just had a beautiful baby and she thought you would like to see her. The baby's name is Hyacinth Maximusa – we named her after you! Can you come and see them both before Henrietta has to go home?"

"Sorry, I couldn't possibly," said Maximus. "The sun is just right for sunbathing on my favourite gravestone. I'm going to sunbathe on Dead Ernest right now."

Herbert went off feeling very disappointed that Maximus didn't want to see his beautiful granddaughter. Maximus lay down in the hot sun and went to sleep.

Several hours later the sun hid behind the church tower and the gravestone was left in the shade. Maximus woke up and shivered. He felt like the two taps in a wash basin – both hot and cold at the same time. Part of him was very hot and burning but inside he seemed to be all chilly and shivery. He rolled off Dead Ernest and stumbled towards the church. He was groaning and holding his head and not looking where he was going.

Round the corner of a high gravestone came Johann Sebastian, the organist's cat. The two animals bumped into each other. Maximus, being the smallest, fell flat on the ground.

"Sorry, old chap," said Johann, "but you really should look where you're going. All you all right? You look very red round the whiskers!"

"I feel dreadful," moaned Maximus. "I don't think I can make it back to the vestry."

"I'll give you a ride," said the cat. "Climb up on my back. I'll soon have you home in bed."

In next to no time Maximus was lying in his bed. The cat had found some cream to put on his sunburn and Maximus was feeling better already. As he lay there he said to himself, "I don't deserve this. Johann Sebastian has been so kind to me but I didn't help anybody. Poor Patrick and Paula couldn't go to see Willy and the Whisker Bangers, Barnabas couldn't go to the hospital and Herbert only wanted me to see his granddaughter. I have not been a very nice mouse today."

Maximus jumped out of bed and scampered across to the Sunday School cupboard.

"Quick," he said, "I've come to mouseling sit. Go and enjoy the music."

Final Comment: It's very easy to think about ourselves – it's much harder to put other people first.

Prayer

Father God,
It is very easy to be selfish – to think of ourselves
before we think of others. Help us to put other
people first and ourselves last. Amen

Hymn

65   When I needed a neighbour
75   I saw the man from Galilee
70   Would you walk by
71   If I had a hammer

12 MAXIMUS HIBERNATES

Theme: Laziness

Aim: To show that good things can be missed if we are lazy

Preparation: The notice that Maximus put on the door of the vestry

Story

It was very quiet in the vestry. Outside the birds were singing, the wind was whistling because he was happy, and the sun was playing hide and seek in and out of the clouds. Inside it seemed as though nothing was moving. In fact unless you got very close to the tiny tissue duvet in one corner you might think that there was no one there at all. But if you were to lay the tip of one finger, very gently, on the duvet you would feel an up and down sort of movement. The sort that means that there might just be some small creature breathing slowly. The creature was a mouse called Maximus.

If you had walked through the church towards the vestry you might have seen a small scrap of paper pinned to the bottom of the door. If you had then bent right down low you could have read these words:

I HAM IBIN8ING
sined
MAXIMUS
PS DO KNOT DISTUB

Patrick, Maximus's best friend, read the notice and walked straight in. He went over to the snoring figure under the duvet.

"Maximus," he said, "Paula and I are going to the sale in Barks and Dentures. They've got lots of bargains. Do you want to come with us?"

The sleeping figure gave a grunt. The duvet moved a fraction and spoke.

"Go away. Can't you read? I'm asleep."

"Oh, all right then, but we thought you might like to come shopping."

And Patrick tip-pawed away. Half an hour later there was the noise of flapping wings in the church. It was Barnabas, the church bat, who lived in the belfry. He swooped low, straight through the door, and landed upside down, clinging to the vicar's coathanger.

"Maximus, my dormant rodent companion, I am visiting an emporium of great educational expectation this very day – namely the Battish

Museum. I would consider it both a pleasure and an honour should you accompany me on this academic expedition."

The figure under the duvet poked a nose and whiskers outside the duvet and grunted again. The whiskers twitched and there was a loud sneeze.

"Go away. Can't you read? I'm asleep."

"Oh, very well. What a Philistine you are. Education is obviously wasted on mice," said Barnabas.

He flew away disturbing the dust once more. Another sneeze followed the first and the duvet lay still.

At the time when Maximus would normally be chasing around looking for something to eat for lunch, another visitor appeared. It was a very prickly ball with little black feet and a small black snout. The prickly ball was Herbert, one of the hedgehogs that lived in the churchyard.

"Maximus, dear old friend, I come with an invitation," said the hedgehog. "We are having a birthday party today for my granddaughter Hyacinth. Her mother has cooked all sorts of delicious delicacies – there are ants in custard, earthworm spaghetti and rotten apple pie. Do please come. All the family would love to see you."

There was a slight movement beneath the duvet and, if the old hedgehog's hearing had been better, he would have recognised the smacking together of mousy lips.

"Go away. Can't you read? I'm asleep," said the duvet.

A little later, just after school time, a furry figure

bounced into the vestry and over to the duvet. It had large stuck up ears and a sort of ball of cotton wool at the back. It was Robin, the youngest son of Robert and Roberta, all of whom lived in a burrow in the churchyard.

"Maximus, good buddy," said Robin, "just where are you at? We had a date with a pawball. We need you between the posts. Come on Max – like now."

The duvet shivered. No more than the tip of a whiskered nose poked out.

"Go away. Can't you read? I'm asleep."

The young rabbit hopped off to play leaving the duvet to go back to sleep.

About the time that the sun rested his head on a large white cloud and went to sleep, the duvet moved. First, it went up in the air like a tent, and then it fell again like a burst balloon. Maximus appeared from under the duvet and stretched his front legs and then his back legs. He yawned and spoke to the empty vestry.

"It must be the spring. Time for all hibernating animals to get up and eat."

He walked into the church. Coming from under the Sunday School cupboard door was the most whisker twitching, nose grabbing smell. It was more than a smell. It was pure delight.

"That's...er, confetti hotpot with candlewax chips and is there some...? Er, yes definitely, organic music sauce," sighed Maximus to the empty church.

The smell drew Maximus closer to the Sunday School cupboard door. After another long sniff he knocked on it.

"Oh, woken up, have we?" asked Paula. "Don't tell me, I know, you've sniffed supper. Come on in then."

"I've been hibernating," said Maximus.

"Rubbish!" said Patrick. "YOU HAVE BEEN LAZY! You've stayed in bed doing nothing but sleep. Well, you missed lots of bargains at Barks and Dentures and, from what we've heard, a very good party for baby Hyacinth Hedgehog."

"And Barnabas told me he had a brilliant day at the Battish Museum," added Paula. "Robin was saying that they had found a new goalkeeper for their pawball team."

"Oh dear," said Maximus, "perhaps hibernating isn't a good thing for mice."

"Being lazy isn't a good thing for mice!" said Patrick and Paula together.

Final Comment: We will never make the most of ourselves if we are lazy.

Prayer
Lord Jesus,
It's very easy to spend our time doing nothing.
Teach us that we miss out on so much when we are lazy. Help us to do the best for ourselves and for others and to use time sensibly. Amen

Hymn
45   The journey of life
49   We are climbing Jesus' ladder
47   One more step along the world I go

13 YOU CAN'T BE SOMEMOUSE ELSE

Theme: We are who we are

Aim: To think about making the most of who we are – not wishing to be someone else.

Preparation: Fit paper wings to your Maximus

Story

"Wait! Stop! Hold it!" shouted Patrick. "MAXIMUS! WHAT ARE YOU DOING?"

Patrick came into the church from the Sunday School cupboard. As he looked around he saw Maximus; at least he thought it was Maximus. His friend was balancing on his rear paws on the edge of the pulpit. Stuck to each paw was a page from a hymnbook, folded in the shape of a bat's wing.

As Patrick was about to shout again, Maximus yelled 'Geronimouse!' and launched himself into space. Patrick covered his eyes with his paws and waited for the crash. What he heard was more of a splash than a crash. After a moment of silence the brave airmouse squeaked.

"Help! Get me out of here. I'm drowning ... glug, glug, glug."

Patrick scampered round to the front of the pulpit and saw what had happened. Maximus had been very lucky. He had landed in a large vase of chrysanthemums, breaking both his fall and the flowers at the same time. His paper wings were soaking up the water and getting in the way of his attempts to climb out.

After a lot of effort, and some help from Patrick, Maximus was on dry land. Patrick noticed that Maximus had chosen the hymn 'For those in peril on the sea' for one of his wings.

"Thanks, Patrick," said Maximus scratching his head and shaking the water from his fur. "Something went wrong. I think it was the shape of the wings. I shall have to look at Barnabas more closely."

"Maximus, what are you trying to do?"

"Not trying to 'do'," said Maximus, "but trying to 'be'. I am going to fly. If bats and birds can do it then so can any self-respecting mouse. It's a question of aerodynamite. Now, back to the drawing board."

"But Maximus," pleaded Patrick, "bats are meant to fly – MICE ARE NOT! You will end up hurting yourself. You could even kill yourself if you are not careful. Please don't ever try it again. Go back to the vestry and put on some dry clothes. Be happy being a mouse."

...

The two friends didn't meet for several days. Patrick was beginning to wonder if Maximus was all right when there was a loud bang on the Sunday School cupboard door.

"Quick! Come quickly please," begged a young rabbit. It was Robin, Robert and Roberta's youngest. "It's Maximus. He's got himself stuck underground."

Patrick rushed out of the church and there, near the church gate, was a crowd of very worried looking rabbits and hedgehogs. They were standing around a small deep hole but when they saw Patrick they all started to talk at once.

"Maximus is down..."

"He's stuck and he can't..."

"He borrowed my best spade and then..."

"Don't know how we can get him..."

"Please wait everybody!" shouted Patrick. "Robert, tell me what's happened."

"Well," said Robert, "Maximus came early this morning and borrowed my spade. He said something about 'if rabbits can live in burrows then so can mice.' He wouldn't listen to me when I told him rabbits is rabbits and mice is mice."

"Right," said Patrick. "Quiet everyone. Let's see if we can hear anything."

He put his ear to the top of the hole. All the hedgehogs and mice were quite still. After a short time Patrick could just hear a very faint squeak.

"Get... me... out. I'm... stu... ck."

"Now listen to me," said Patrick, climbing to the top of the pile of earth dug from the hole.

"Herbert, organise your hedgehogs to dig over there. Robert, you and your family dig this side. One of the two tunnels should reach Maximus. We can't go in behind him or the earth will fall in and cover him up."

The two rescue teams started to dig furiously. Soon there were two piles of earth and stones and roots on either side of Maximus's hole. Both teams changed diggers every few minutes. Patrick kept calling down to Maximus to tell him what was happening. Time went on and it began to get dark. Paula and some of the mouselings went to fetch candles from the church.

It was Horatio, Herbert's son-in-law, that was the first to reach the little mouse. He was deep in the tunnel when he heard a faint squeak. As he scraped away more earth Maximus tumbled into Horatio's tunnel. Then another tunnel broke through and Richard, Robert's oldest son, appeared. With Richard pushing and Horatio dragging they soon had Maximus out of the tunnel and into the open. Paula rushed over to him and gave him a big hug and then a drink.

"I was only trying to be a rabbit," said Maximus to Patrick the next day. "I thought if rabbits could live in burrows then mice might try it. It would have been less draughty than the church."

"Maximus, you've tried flying like a bat. You've tried digging like a rabbit. Why don't you realise that you are a mouse? Mice don't fly. Mice do not dig tunnels. Mice do mousy things. When they try to do other things they hurt themselves and make a lot of trouble for other animals who have to rescue them."

"Yes, I know you're right. But sometimes I wish I was somebody else," said Maximus. "I did think I might see what being a water rat was like…"

"DON'T YOU DARE!" warned Patrick.

Final Comment: We cannot change who we are but we can make the most of ourselves.

Prayer
God our Creator,
You have made us as we are. Help us to make the
very best of ourselves without worrying about being
different. Help us to work and play as well as we
can so that we enjoy being ourselves. Amen

Hymn
64   The wise may bring their learning
113   A time to be born
3   All things bright and beautiful
5   Carpenter, carpenter, make me a tree
15   There are hundreds of sparrows

14 SAINTS DON'T LIVE IN STAINED GLASS WINDOWS

Theme: Good examples

Aim: To thank God for those who make our lives better

Preparation: A stained glass window drawn on an overhead projector acetate or made from greaseproof paper

Story

The sun had got out of bed in a very good mood. It had decided to shine all day without a break. There was not a cloud in the sky and the wind had gone on holiday as well.

A small mouse was wandering about St Michael's Church looking for something to eat. The mouse stopped, sat down, and scratched his head. There was something odd, something different, about the colour of the floor. Normally it was grey, with darker lines where the large stones met. Now it was... well, it was red and blue and green and brown and yellow and black and some more colours that the mouse couldn't name.

Maximus, who was the mouse sitting in the pool of colour, just couldn't understand it at all. Someone had been in the church when he wasn't looking and painted the floor in all those colours. How dare they? What would everyone think? He tried scratching the colours with his front claws but it made no difference. He got a bucket of water and a cloth and scrubbed as hard as he could but the colours stayed.

"It could be one of Patrick and Paula's mouselings," he muttered to the empty church. "Mouselings," he went on, "they just don't care today. No respect for anyone or anything. It's what they call giraffeety – that's what it is."

Maximus scurried up the church and stopped in front of the Sunday School cupboard. He knocked as hard as he could on the door.

"Hello, Maximus," said Patrick yawning. "Sorry but we overslept this morning. Is there something you want?"

"I want to know who done it!" shouted Maximus. "One of your juvenile detergents has painted the church floor – not just one colour but lots. It's a disgrace."

"Hold on, Maximus. You'll burst a button off your shirt if you're not careful. Now, tell me calmly, what's happened."

"Parents should be responsible for their

mouselings. That's what I say."

"Maximus, I don't know what you're talking about."

"There!" pointed Maximus. "There's lots of paint on the floor."

"All right, I'll come and look," said a puzzled Patrick.

The two mice walked through the church until they came to the colours on the floor.

"That's funny," said Maximus, "but it's moved a little bit. It was nearer the pillar before. Are you sure your mouselings aren't playing games in the church?"

"They're all at home," said Patrick, "not one of them is out. It must be someone else. Come and have some Maxwell Mouse coffee. Then we'll go and ask Barnabas if he's seen anything."

Barnabas is the church bat who lives in the belfry, which he calls the battery. He is a very wise bat who normally sleeps all day and wakes up at night. In the summer he eats crickets and grasshoppers, which is why his nickname is the Cricket Bat. Maximus and Patrick climbed the stairs to the belfry with difficulty. They were out of breath when they reached the top.

"Er... excuse us, please, Barnabas," said Maximus, "but we have a problem."

"It is only when some problematical event occurs that you present yourselves in my campanile. I imagine that it is your anticipation that I shall be able to solve the current conundrum?"

"Er... yes, I think so," said a rather confused

Maximus. "You see we have a secret floor painter in the church who comes and paints colours and then they move and then after a bit they move again and Patrick says it isn't any of his."

"Your presentation of the predicament is such that I have less than a totally clear comprehension of the issue you are posing. However, it is my experience that your saintly named companion is generally better equipped to offer a satisfactory explanation."

"He means you, Patrick," whispered Maximus.

...

Ten minutes later two mice and one bat could be seen looking closely at the colours on the church floor. The patch of colour had moved again during their visit to the belfry.

"Saints alight!" exclaimed Barnabas.

"Pardon?" stammered Maximus and Patrick together.

"The juxtaposition of the solar orb in conjunction with the multi-coloured fenestration has projected the colours contained in the stained glass window."

"I think what he means is that the sun is shining through the stained glass window. You know, the window with St Peter and St Paul in it," said Patrick.

The mice turned and looked. Sure enough the bright sunlight was shining through the large window with the picture of the two saints. Because the angle of the sun changed through the day, the colours moved slowly round the church floor.

"I see that comprehension has dawned," said Barnabas, and he flew back to the belfry.

"I often wondered what saints were for," said Maximus. "Now I know. They let light and colour into dark places."

"You don't have to live in a stained glass window to do that," said Patrick. "There are lots of people, and mice, that make dark things brighter."

"I think that's what Jesus does," said Maximus thoughtfully. "If you look in the other window there is a picture of Jesus. The words underneath say, 'I am the light of the world. Whoever follows me will have the light of life and never walk in darkness.'"

Final Comment: Our lives are better because many people have let in the light.

Prayer
Father God,
Thank you for all those that make dark days brighter. Help us to follow Jesus, who came to bring light into a dark world, and to reflect his light to others. Amen

Hymn
23   Jesus good above all other
63   You inspired men, long, long ago
55   Colours of day dawn into the mind
53   Peace, perfect peace
47   One more step along the world I go

15 READ THE INSTRUCTIONS

Theme: The Bible

Aim: To show the Bible is a special book

Preparation: Have a Bible and a manual (car, washing machine, etc) to show the children

Story

One moment it was there. The next moment it had gone. Maximus sat for a few seconds in total darkness, hoping it would come back. He expected a voice to say, 'We are very sorry about the loss of picture but it is due to a fault at the transmitter.' But nothing happened.

Maximus had been in the middle of watching one of his favourite programmes *Mouse Party*, in which famous mice were interviewed and chose a piece of music. Willy, of Willy and the Whisker Bangers, had just chosen Gerry and the Gerbils to sing their current hit, when the television went dead.

Maximus lit a candle and made sure that the plug hadn't fallen out of the socket on the wall. He kicked the set with his front paws but that didn't make any difference either. There was nothing for it – he needed help. He scurried across the church to the Sunday School cupboard. Patrick and Paula and the mouselings were still watching *Mouse Party*.

"Come in Maximus," said Patrick, "shan't be a minute. We're just enjoying *Mouse Party*. I thought this was one of your favourite programmes?"

"It is," said Maximus, "it's just a bit difficult to see it on a blank screen!"

They watched the end of the programme and Paula sent the mouselings off to bed with a cup of Morelicks each.

"What's the problem?" asked Patrick.

"My set's upset," said Maximus. "It's ill. It won't work. I missed the best bit of *Mouse Party* because it went black."

"Sounds serious," said Patrick. "I'll come and have a look."

The two mice scampered back to the vestry and Maximus re-lit the candle. Patrick unplugged the set from the wall and unscrewed the back. As he did so his whiskers twitched and he sneezed several times.

"When did you dust this last?"

"I think it was this year," said Maximus laughing. "Might not have been."

"Well, I can't see anything wrong. Television is really clever, isn't it? There are mice all over the world and we can see what they're doing. We can even see what goes on in the Mouse of Commons."

"But what am I going to do?" asked Maximus anxiously. "It'll be *Coronation Mouseholes* tomorrow night. I can't miss that."

"I think we may have to ask Barnabas in the morning," replied his friend. "Barnabas is really clever – he'll know what to do. Now I'm off to bed."

The next morning Barnabas was hanging upside down on a bell rope when the two mice climbed into the belfry.

"Oh no!" said Barnabas rather rudely. "It's Minibus and Peastick, the revolting rodents come to disturb my sleep. I anticipate a problem requiring my superior brain power."

"Please, Mr Barnabas, we're really sorry to bother you but we need your advice. You see Maximus's telly isn't working. It's gone black."

"And I can't hear anything either," Maximus joined in.

"Is it essential that you disturb my nocturnal aspirations on a Sunday morning simply because your inferior electronic device has failed? We bats have used electronic devices for millions of years. We are undoubtedly the most advanced of all creatures. Have you considered consulting the manufacturer's almanac? Their Instruction Manuals often provide the solutions to these technical enigmas."

"That's it," said Patrick. "We should have looked at the book that came with the set, Maximus."

Barnabas was asleep before the two mice had crept out of the belfry. Back in the vestry they found a book with the title *Rodent Rentals Television Set – Mark Five.*

"That's the one, look in there," said Maximus, who wasn't the best reader of the two. "What does it say?"

"Page Six – Faults," read Patrick.

1   *Make sure the power is getting to the set.*
2   *Make sure all the switches are turned on.*
3   *Check no wires have become loose inside the set. Before doing this you must unplug the set from the power supply.*

"It must be a loose wire," said Patrick. "We've checked all the other things. Hand me the screwdriver please."

Patrick disappeared into the back of the television set and started to sneeze again. After a few minutes Maximus heard a muffled squeak.

"I've found it. Should be all right again now."

Patrick backed out of the television set covered in dust. They screwed the back on, pushed in the plug, and turned it on. Almost at once they heard a voice. It was the Sunday Service. The minister was speaking to the children.

"Sometimes," he said, "our toys go wrong. Perhaps the computer won't work or the gears on your mountain bike won't change. What do you do then? It's usually a question of asking Dad or Mum to fix it. When all else fails, they read the Instruction Manual.

"But sometimes things go wrong in our lives. We

do wrong things. We get cross and angry or we get into trouble because we take something which isn't ours. Often we don't seem to be able to make it better on our own. It's then we need the special Instruction Manual that God has given us. It's called the Bible. It's full of very good advice on how to live our lives so things don't go wrong AND what to do when they do. If you read some every day you'll find it makes a big difference."

"Fancy that," said Maximus. "Humans have an Instruction Manual like my telly. I hope they read it!"

Final Comment: The Bible tells us a lot about God and a lot about ourselves.

Prayer
Heavenly Father,
Thank you for the Bible, for all that we can read about you in it, and for all that it can teach us about ourselves. Help us when we read it to understand what you are telling us and then help us to do it.
Amen

Hymn
100 I may speak in the tongues of angels
108 The Lord, the Lord is my shepherd
81   What about being old Moses?
56   The Lord's my shepherd

16 FINDERS AREN'T ALWAYS KEEPERS

Theme: Honesty

Aim: To explore the meaning of ownership

Preparation: A purse

Story

Maximus opened his purse, shook it, and waited for the sound of falling coins. There was silence. Nothing came out. It was what he was afraid of – he was broke. There was no other way to describe it.

He had been to the sales and spent all his money. He had bought a new duvet, a CD player, and some new CDs to go with it. His favourite group was called Hard Cheese and their new CD was very expensive. He especially liked the track with the words:

'*Eat it, beat it, meet it, Hard Cheese;*
Cheat for it, bleat for it, don't ever delete it;
Hard Cheese.'

In fact Maximus played it so often that Patrick wouldn't come into the vestry when it was on. But all this spending had left him without any money – not even enough to buy food. Having had no breakfast and no lunch he went round to see Patrick and Paula.

"I don't suppose you could lend me some money?" he asked. "You see, I need to go shopping, and it's sort of disappeared."

"You mean you've spent it all," said Paula.

"Hard Cheese!" said Patrick.

"That's not very nice," said Maximus. "I ask you politely if I can borrow some money and all you can say is 'hard cheese'."

"'Hard Cheese' are the problem, Maximus," said Patrick, with a grin. "If you hadn't bought their CD you might have enough money to buy food."

"Oh, I see what you mean," said Maximus, "but ... er, I am rather hungry."

"Of course you can borrow some," said Paula, and she gave Maximus some coins from her purse. "I can't lend you much. We've got to get some new shoes for the mouselings tomorrow."

"Thanks," said Maximus. "I'll let you have it back as soon as I can."

Maximus always walked through the park to the Wasda Supermarket. There was a pretty lake in the park and Maximus usually stopped and had a chat with the ducks. Today there was nobody about. No ducks, no squirrels, no moles, nobody to be seen at all. Maximus, whose tummy was beginning to rumble, scampered by the lake and headed towards the gate opposite the supermarket.

Suddenly he stopped. Had he really seen it or had he dreamt it? No, he was right. It was there, on the edge of the rose bed. A large black purse! Maximus looked around to check there was no one else in the park. He picked it up. It felt quite heavy. There must be lots of money in it. He looked around again, just to make sure. Surely it wouldn't do any harm to see how much was in it?

It was full of ten pound notes. There must have been at least twenty of them. Maximus couldn't believe it. Two hundred pounds. He'd never seen so much in his life. Two hundred pounds would last him for weeks. He could buy more CDs. He might even manage to go to the next Hard Cheese gig. It was what he had always wanted – to see Hard Cheese and get their pawgraphs. Maximus dropped the purse inside his empty Wasda bag.

He was rich. He was richer than he ever thought possible. Or was he? Was it his to keep? If he had found it, then someone had lost it. Fancy losing all that money! Of course it wouldn't be a problem if you had lots – but what if you hadn't? What if this money was all someone had?

What should he do? He could go to Wasda and buy all those things he really loved – a big bag of ant flavoured crisps, a piece of Cheddar cheese twice his own size, some wax waffles, some chocolate mousse (or should it be chocolate mice?), and lots more. Or ... he could give the purse back. Hand it in at a police station.

Maximus started to cross the road towards Wasda. He was thinking so hard that he nearly got knocked over by two frogs on mountain bikes.

"Wake up, you dozy mouse!" shouted one of the frogs. "Not safe out on your own, you aren't."

It was a case of toad rage and Maximus ignored them. He took a trolley from the trolley park and walked in towards the checkout. As he got nearer he heard some loud voices.

"You must pay for it," said the girl hedgehog sitting at the checkout. "If you can't pay then I shall have to get the Manager."

Standing by the checkout and frantically searching her bag was an old duck. She was looking very worried and frightened. Her voice was quite quacked.

"But it was here. I know it was here," she said. "I never go out without my purse."

"Well, where is it?" said the checkout hedgehog. Other animals in the queue were beginning to grumble. "I can't keep all these waiting."

"I don't know," sobbed the duck. "If I've lost it, then I've lost everything. All the money I have. I was taking it to the bank – to the River Bank."

"I'm sorry you've lost your money," said the girl hedgehog, "but you'll just have to put all these things back where you got them from."

The duck began to reload her trolley. Maximus stood there watching her. All that money belonged to her. She must have lost the purse when she came out of the park.

"It's ... er, all right," said Maximus, walking over to the checkout. He took the purse from his bag. "I think this must be yours," he said to the old duck.

...

"It would have been very easy to keep it," said Maximus, later that day, to Patrick and Paula. "But I am very glad I didn't."

"How about having supper with us?" said Paula. "We're having confetti soup and roast hymn book cover."

Final Comment: Remind the children about school rules on finding things and of the importance of not touching things they might find out of school.

Prayer
Loving Father,
Sometimes we see things that don't belong to us and we want them. Help us to be honest in all things and remember that what doesn't belong to us does belong to someone else.

Hymn
62 Heavenly Father, may thy blessing
103 The road of life lies before
57 Think of all the things we lose
89 Guess how I feel

17   OPEN UNIVERSITY

Theme: Try hard to get it right

Aim: To encourage children not to give up too easily

Preparation: A certificate for Maximus

Story
Maximus stood waiting by the vestry door. Why was the post always late when he wanted something to come? At that moment a large brown envelope fell through the letterbox. Maximus tore it open and read the following letter.

Dear Mr Maximus Mouse,

Thank you for your letter and for returning your application form for Mousebridge Open University. I am pleased to inform you that you have been accepted as a student on the Creative Writing Course.

I shall be your tutor for the Course. Please complete the first piece of written work and return it to me by the end of the month.

May I take this opportunity to wish you well for all your studies.

Yours sincerely,

Professor William Shakepaw

Maximus rushed out of the vestry and over to the Sunday School cupboard.

"Patrick," he shouted, "it's come! I've had a letter from Professor Shakepaw. I'm a student of Mousebridge Open University."

"Mine's come too!" said Patrick, waving his envelope at Maximus. "We've both been accepted."

The two mice had talked about becoming students for ages and finally Paula, who was tired of listening to them, told them to apply.

"Now you can show the mouselings what hard work is really like," she said. "Why don't you make a start on your first project?"

"Write a short poem about being a mouse," read Maximus. "You must imagine that it will be read by a human who has no idea how a mouse feels."

They sat for a long time gazing at the blank sheets of white paper in front of them. Maximus chewed the end of his pencil and Patrick started to nibble the paper. At last they both started writing. Patrick put his paw in front of his poem so that Maximus couldn't see it.

"Read it to me, Patrick," said Maximus. "Go on, please."

Patrick coughed and started to read.

'Mice' by Patrick Mouse
I have always been a mouse,
I was born a mouse in my mother's house.
I have mousy hair and a mousy tail,
And I'm really glad I'm not a whale.

I think mousy thoughts, both day and night,
If I see a cat I have a mousy fright.
My wife is a mousy wife –
And I shall stay a mouse all my life."

"That's brilliant," said Maximus. "Now let me read you mine.

'Maximus Mouse' by Maximus Mouse
I have known me all my life,
From the day that I was born.
I have never been anyone else –
From dawn to dawn to dawn.

A mouse I am, a mouse I shall stay,
Whatever anyone does or whatever they may say.
From tip of my nose to end of my tail –
I am mouse all the way through, without fail."

"Amazing," said Patrick, "just amazing. We've written our first poems. That Professor Shakepaw will be so pleased with us."

"He might give us our certifimice now," said Maximus. "I'm sure when he sees how clever we are he won't expect us to write anymore. Come on, let's put the poems in the post."

Patrick and Maximus scampered off to the pillar-box and posted their work back to Professor Shakepaw. A week later they got replies.

Dear Mr Maximus,

Thank you for sending me your poem entitled 'Maximus Mouse' by Maximus Mouse. I regret to say that this is of a very poor standard and I seriously question whether you should continue with the Course. This university takes its Creative Writing standards very seriously, which is more than you appear to have done, with the absurd poem you submitted. I can only assume that it was intended as a misplaced joke.

I am prepared to give you one more chance. Your assignment is to write a poem to describe the finest cheddar cheese you have ever eaten.

I have written to Mr Patrick Mouse along similar lines, as it appears that you consult one another over your work. I hope there will be an immediate improvement in your work.

Yours sincerely,

Professor William Shakepaw

Maximus, for once in his life, was squeakless. He could not believe that anyone could write to him like that. Well, that was it – there was not going to be any more. Professor Shakepaw could find other students. He was obviously a man who simply did not recognise good poetry when he saw it.

At that moment Patrick came into the vestry carrying his letter from Professor Shakepaw.

"I don't think he liked it!" said Patrick.

"He didn't," shouted Maximus, "and I don't like him! I'm not wasting my time writing poetry for him any more."

"I feel the same," said Patrick, "but Paula thinks we should try again. She says now we can only get better. She said something about it's easy to give up but much harder to carry on. She also said something about us setting an example to the mouselings."

"She's a hard mouse, that wife of yours!" said Maximus. "I mean how would she feel if it had happened to her?"

"Well, I'm going to try again," said Patrick. "Why don't you do the same?"

"I'll think about it," said Maximus.

Patrick went back home to the Sunday School cupboard and Maximus threw himself onto his duvet. By the next morning he had calmed down. Perhaps his poetry wasn't brilliant after all. Perhaps he did need some help. Perhaps he could do better. He sat down and tried again. This time he thought about what he wanted to write. He wrote it down, read it through and then wrote it again. He did this twice until he was really sure he had written it as well as he could.

Maximus and Patrick put their new poems in the post to Professor Shakepaw without reading each other's work. It took another week before the Professor replied. Maximus tore open the envelope and read the following words:

Dear Mr Maximus Mouse,

I can hardly believe that you are the same student who wrote the poem 'Maximus Mouse'. Your poem about favourite cheddar cheese shows great improvement and I shall be publishing it in the USA the end of term.

Congratulations and keep up the good work.

Yours sincerely,

Professor William Shakepaw

PS. USA stands for University Students' Anthology.

Maximus went to supper that evening with Patrick and Paula. The professor had also been pleased with Patrick's poem.

"You see, it only goes to show, you can do things if you put some effort into them," said Paula. "Now, Maximus, you must read me your poem."

And this is the poem that Maximus read.

Cheddar Cheese and the Five Senses
To smell, and taste, and then to touch,
To hear and see, it is too much,
When thinking of that rare delight –
A piece of Cheddar cheese tonight.

The smell is finer than perfume,
Than any rose that is in bloom;
The taste puts chocolate in the shade
It's worth however much you paid!

The silky touch when paw meets cheese,
Is guaranteed to more than please;
O listen as it speaks to you
Of quality that's always true.

To see it, is the greatest pleasure,
To regard it at my leisure
And let my senses dwell at ease
Upon my favourite Cheddar Cheese.

Final Comment: Reading through and re-drafting
are hard work but they are worthwhile if
afterwards you have written a better story or poem.

Prayer
Heavenly Father,
Help us to understand that everything we do, must
be the best we can do. In our work at school, in the
games we play and in our love for you, help us to
give only the best.

Hymn
86   The bell of creation is swinging for ever
87   Give us hope, Lord, for each day
42   Travel on, travel on
43   Give me oil in my lamp
45   The journey of life
47   One more step along the world I go

PARABLES

18 MAXIMUS MEETS A GOOD SAMARITAN

Theme: True friends

Aim: To consider the meaning of true friendship

Preparation: A Bible: to show the origin of the story in Luke 10:25–37

Story

"Hello Patrick, hi Paula," said Maximus. "Welcome to my party. Find yourselves something to eat."

Maximus was having a party on the grass near the church car park. It was a beautiful summer's evening and lots of his friends had come. They were eating and chatting to each other and really enjoying themselves. Robert and Roberta Rabbit were there; so too were several hedgehogs, bats and mice.

Patrick and Paula are Maximus's oldest friends, and had helped Maximus get ready by making the hymn sheet sandwiches, the organic music quiche and the confetti and rice dips.

Maximus scurried around talking to his guests and making sure that they had enough to eat and drink. He stopped next to Patrick and Paula.

"Seems to be going well, don't you think?" he asked.

"Very," said Paula. "Can't see Desmond and Daphne though. Have they come?"

"Well, er … no," said Maximus. "To be honest, I didn't invite them. You see, they're harvest mice. Not quite the same as us house mice. Not quite so, well … er … educated. I thought they might not want to come, so I didn't invite them."

"Maximus! I'm very disappointed in you," said Paula. "Oh, well, it's too late now."

The rest of the evening went off very happily and all the animals enjoyed themselves and were late going home. Several stayed behind to help Maximus clear up and it was nearly midnight before they had finished.

The others had gone and Maximus was having a last look round when he heard a swishing noise. Before he could say 'hymn sheet sandwich', he was airborne. That is to say, he was held tight in the sharp claws of an owl. The owl, who fancied mice pudding for his supper, was flying back to his nest. The nest was high up in one of the trees that surround the churchyard.

Maximus was absolutely terrified. He wriggled and scratched and shouted. He tried to hit the owl with his front paws and kick it with his back paws at the same time.

At last he was free. Free falling that is! He was falling very quickly back down into the churchyard. Maximus landed in the middle of the churchyard rubbish tip. It was the heap of dead grass and leaves that gave him a soft landing. All the breath was knocked out of him. He lay there very still. Then he started to check if everything was still working. He wriggled his ears and then his whiskers – they were all right. He wriggled each leg in turn and checked each paw. When he got to his front left leg he knew things were not good. The leg was hurting and his paw was cut. He couldn't move and he badly needed help but he was afraid to squeak too loudly in case the owl found him again.

After what seemed like ages he heard a snuffling, shuffling sort of noise. The snout of a short-sighted hedgehog poked through the leaves which covered Maximus.

"Oh dear," it said, "a mouse asleep on the tip. Probably had too much to drink!"

And the hedgehog went off to find something to eat. A few moments later a rat passed by, but didn't stop when it saw Maximus.

"Some creatures just can't look after themselves," muttered the rat.

Maximus was quite sure that no one was ever going to help him. He would be found dead the next day on the rubbish tip. He lay there feeling very sorry for himself. Just when he had finally given up hope there was a rustle in the rotting leaves.

"Are you all right?" asked a small voice. "Can I help?"

"Yes please," said Maximus. "You see, I've hurt my leg and I can't move."

The owner of the kind voice crept nearer. It had whiskers, bright eyes and brown fur. It was a harvest mouse. In fact, it was Desmond, out late, searching for food for his mouselings. Maximus couldn't believe how fortunate he had been. In a very short while he was tucked up in his bed, his leg was bandaged, and he was drifting off to sleep. And all because of Desmond and his family.

The next Sunday morning, Maximus was in church for the Family Service. His leg was healing well and he was feeling a lot better. The vicar started to read from the Bible.

"Our reading today is from Luke's Gospel, chapter ten. This is the story that Jesus told so that people would learn that everyone is their neighbour," he said, "not just the people we pick and choose." And he read the story about the Good Samaritan.

Maximus could hardly believe his furry ears. The story that Jesus told was just like what happened to him. He hadn't been very friendly towards the harvest mice. He hadn't invited them to his party. But it was the harvest mice that had helped him. They had helped him when other animals had left him alone.

That evening Maximus planned another party, smaller than the first, for just a few friends. It was for his new friends – Desmond and Daphne and their mouselings.

Final comment: Think about the friends you have and make friends with those who don't have any.

Prayer
Heavenly Father,
It is easy to be nice to people we know and like.
Help us to be friends to all and to remember that we
should love our neighbours as we love ourselves.
Amen

Hymn
47   One more step along the world I go
65   When I needed a neighbour
70   Would you walk by on the other side?
90   I come like a beggar with a gift in my hand
88   I was lying in the roadway

19 LOST AND FOUND

Theme: We are never really lost

Aim: To show how Jesus used stories to teach us about the love of God

Preparation: Show a book that has a lost and found theme.

A Bible: to show the origin of the story in Luke 15:1–7

Story

Maximus lay in the sort of doze when you are half-awake and half-asleep. Suddenly a thought came to him. He leapt out of bed, fell over his slippers, picked himself up and rushed out into the church.

"It's the day!" he shouted. "The special day we've all been waiting for."

He scampered to the Sunday School cupboard. Paula came to the door.

"It's today!" he said. "The tomorrow we were talking about yesterday. Why aren't you ready?"

"What is the matter, Maximus? Why are you jumping around in the church in your pyjamas? What's all this shouting about?"

"But it's your special day, Paula," said Maximus. "It's your wedding anniversary."

He rushed over to Paula, clutching his pyjama trousers as he ran, and gave her a big kiss.

"Maximus, what would the children say?" said Paula, rather breathlessly. "Here you are, half naked, squeezing the squeak out of me, and generally making a nuisance of yourself."

Maximus stood there with his paws behind his back, one holding tightly to his pyjama trousers. But Paula hadn't finished.

"Go and get dressed," she continued, "and by the time you're ready we'll be waiting for you."

And with that she turned round and went back into the cupboard from which Maximus heard a lot of tiny squeaks.

Half an hour later, dressed in his best going-to-picnic jeans and M shirt, Maximus knocked on the cupboard door again. The door opened and Maximus took several steps backwards. There, in front of him, was the whole of Patrick and Paula's family – forty-three mouselings.

"Good morning, Uncle Maximus," they chorused together.

"Er ... good morning," answered Maximus. "Are you ready for the picnic?"

"Yes, Uncle Maximus," they said.

Maximus could never understand how it was that Patrick and Paula knew all their children. Forty-three seemed so many. How did they remember their names? Did they know all their birthdays? How did they tell which shoes belonged to which paws? It was all quite beyond Maximus.

The mouselings crowded round Maximus, all trying to be the one who held his paw. Soon their parents had sorted them out so that the older children looked after the younger ones. They made a long procession walking out of the church and into the churchyard.

It was a beautiful spring day and the children scampered off running around the gravestones, playing 'hide and squeak', mouse tag and other games.

"Well, you've got a lovely day for your anniversary," said Maximus to Patrick and Paula. The three grown up mice lay in the sunshine. "It's really great to relax and chat to old friends like this."

After an hour or so they began to feel hungry.

"Nearly time for lunch," said Paula. "Patrick, I think you should start to get the children together. Make sure they wash their paws in that puddle before they sit down."

Paula began to unpack a large bag of tiny cheeseburgers and worm paste sandwiches. Maximus could hear Patrick counting the mouselings.

"Thirty-eight, thirty-nine ... Peregrine do stand still, forty, forty-one, Pomegranate put Prudence down, ... forty-two, er ... where is forty-three? Has anyone seen Percival?" asked Patrick anxiously.

But none of the others had seen him anywhere.

"It would be Percy. He really is the limit. He never does what he's told," joined in Paula. "If any mouseling is going to get lost it will always be Percy."

"Patrick, you and I will search," said Maximus, "while the others stay with Paula."

Patrick and Maximus set off through the long grass that grew between some of the older gravestones. Maximus scrambled up on top of one of them but he couldn't see the missing mouseling. They scampered on a little further and shouted again. There was no answer. Patrick was looking very worried and Maximus tried to comfort him.

"I'm sure we'll find Percy soon," he said. "He's really quite a sensible mouse – he can't be far away."

"I do hope you're right," said Patrick, "there are so many things that can happen to young mice today. He might have been mouseknapped or caught by a cat or even run over."

"Shush! I mean ... listen for a moment. I thought I heard a squeak. It's coming from over there."

Maximus pointed towards the rubbish dump near the churchyard fence. It was full of rotting grass from the mower, stumps of old flowers were sticking out like gelled hair, and the smell was terrible. They held their paws to their noses as they started to climb over the rubbish.

"Percival!" shouted Patrick, "Percy, are you

there?"

They listened hard for a reply. There was a tiny squeak.

"Dad, Dad ... I'm down here. Please get me out."

It took Patrick and Maximus quite a long time to move all the leaves and twigs so that they could rescue Percy. At last he was free and they scampered back to a very worried Paula.

"Come on all of you, we've found Percy so let's celebrate," said Maximus.

All the mouselings joined in and they had a fantastic party. They were so happy that the mouseling that was lost had been found.

Next Sunday Maximus sat in church during the Family Service hoping one of the choirboys would drop a piece of chocolate. Maximus started to take notice when the vicar read the lesson from the Bible. It was the story Jesus told about a lost sheep. A shepherd has a hundred sheep and loses one of them. He searches for it until he finds it. He is so happy when he finds it that he has a party.

"God is happy, like that shepherd," said the vicar, "when someone who has done wrong tells God he is sorry and asks to be forgiven."

"I think I know a little bit how it feels," thought Maximus. "We felt the same when Percy was found."

Final Comment: We've all been lost at one time or another – perhaps we've lost sight of Mum in a supermarket or Dad on a beach. It's a lovely feeling to be found and hugged.

Prayer

Dear God,
Sometimes we feel a long way away from you. Help
us to remember that you are always there with us.
Forgive us for the things we do that make you
unhappy. Amen

Hymn

55   Colours of day
57   Think of all the things we lose
47   One more step along the world I go
87   Give us hope, Lord, for each day
96   A still small voice in the heart of the city
101   In the bustle of the city

20 SANDCASTLES SHOULD BE BUILT ON ROCKS

Theme: Good foundations

Aim: To introduce another parable and to show that Jesus will never fail us

Preparation: Rock and sand and a bucket and spade

A Bible : to show the origin of the story in Luke 6:46–49

Story

"Just what we wanted," said Patrick. "The tide's out and there's lots of sand for the mouselings to play on."

Maximus, Patrick, Paula and the mouselings had just arrived at the seaside and they were walking along the promenade.

"Right," ordered Paula, "down on the beach. Make sure all your shoes and socks are left tidily.

We shall have a swim this afternoon when our lunch has gone down. Older ones please look after younger ones. And Percival, I shall be watching you. One paw out of line and no ice cream!"

The mouselings started to dig in the sand. Prunella and Pomegranate together with Peregrine and Percival wandered down towards the sea.

"We can make a bigger castle than you," boasted Percy. "I mean, you're only girl mice!"

Prunella and Pomegranate looked at each other then nodded their heads.

"You're on," said Prunella. "We'll have a competition."

"Right," said Peregrine, "if yours is biggest you can have our ices but if ours is best..."

"Which it will be," said Percy.

" ... we will have yours."

Both pairs of mice started to dig quickly. The girl mouselings chose a spot where a small flat-topped rock jutted up out of the sand. The boys went nearer to the edge of the sea where the sand was wetter and stuck together better. Both pairs worked very hard. They filled their buckets, tipped them out, flattened the sand and then did it all again.

"Can't wait for TWO ice creams," said Percy, loud enough for the girls to hear. "Look at yours," he said, pointing to the girls' castle, "have you started yet?"

The girls ignored Percy's question and carried on with their work.

"Right," said Pomegranate, "half an hour more then we'll get Uncle Maximus and Mum and Dad to judge which is best."

"Shouldn't bother," said Peregrine, " 'sobvious. Ours is best."

Both pairs worked even harder. Buckets were filled and emptied. The castles got higher and higher. The mouselings got hotter and hotter. The boys had flung off their t-shirts, which were now lying in a little rock pool being nibbled by crabs. The one thing that nobody noticed was that the tide was slowly creeping up the beach.

As the last bucket of sand slid off their castle and onto the beach the boys shouted out, "Finished. Time's up. We've won!"

It certainly looked that the boys' castle was higher than the girls. Peregrine and Percy jumped around punching the air with their paws and shouting, "Yes!"

Percy ran off to find Maximus and his parents.

"Come quick," he said to them.

"Quickly, dear ... we say 'come quickly', not 'come quick'," corrected Paula as Percy tumbled into a deep hole dug by Popsie and Posie. "What's the matter? Are Prunella and Pomegranate all right?"

"Yes, fine Mum, we're all fine," said Percival. "We want you three to come and judge our complication."

"I think you mean 'competition'," said Maximus with a grin. "What sort of competition is it?"

"We, that is me and Percy, bet the girls we could make a bigger castle than them. If we win we get their ice creams!"

Maximus, Patrick and Paula followed Percy over the beach, dotted with little holes dug by the rest of the family, towards the two castles. Percy was dancing around them and soon Peregrine joined in.

"So we have to judge which castle is the highest, do we?" asked Maximus.

"Yes, Uncle Maximus, but we're the best," shouted the two boy mouselings together.

The adult mice went over to look at the castle built by Pomegranate and Prunella. It was spread well over the little rock and looked very strong. There were flags on each corner and it was about three buckets high.

"Well done," said Paula. "You've worked very hard but now let's have a look at the boys' castle."

Suddenly Percy gave a loud scream. The adults turned round just in time. A wave broke over the boys' castle and knocked it flat. It was as if it had never been there. The beach was as flat as it had been before they started.

They all sang in the coach going home – apart, that is, from Percival and Peregrine who were not happy mouselings.

...

The next Sunday morning Maximus was, as usual, in church.

Just as he had found a cough sweet stuck to the floor under the organist's stool he heard the vicar reading from the Bible.

" 'Anyone who hears these words of mine,' said Jesus, 'and obeys them is like a wise man that built his house on rock.' The words of Jesus are like a rock in a stormy sea," the vicar went on. "Whatever happens to us, if we cling to those words, we shall never fall. It's a bit like building two sandcastles – one on a rock and one on the beach and watching what happens when the tide comes in."

"I know what you mean," whispered Maximus to himself.

Final Comment: Jesus told his stories a long time ago but they mean just as much to us today.

Prayer
Heavenly Father,
Thank you for the stories that Jesus told. Help us to understand his words and to obey them at all times so that our lives might be built on the rock that is Jesus. Amen

Hymn
47   One more step along the world I go
52   Lord of all hopefulness
22   I danced in the morning
142 I'm gonna lay down my sword and shield

FESTIVALS

21 UNEXPECTED VISITORS

Theme: Christmas

Aim: To remind the children of the coming of Jesus at Christmas

Preparation: A wrapped present

Story

It was Christmas Eve and Maximus couldn't remember a colder Christmas. The wind was blowing hard against the vestry windows and there were flakes of snow in the wind. It was bitterly cold although the heating was on for the Christmas Day services. Maximus had given his presents to Patrick, Paula and the mouselings. He had sent cards to Barnabas the church bat, to Herbert the hedgehog, who lived in the graveyard, and to Robert and his family of rabbits.

Maximus was actually feeling quite proud of himself. For once he was ready for the great day. He had done his shopping and bought all the food he would need. Usually he had Christmas lunch with Patrick and Paula but they had gone away and Maximus was on his own.

There were old films on the television – *Mousy Poppins* about a nursemouse who could do magical things, *The Sound of Mouselings* about a choir of baby mice who lived in Austria and *Snow Black and the Seven Mouselings*. He had seen them all before.

Maximus knew he would be disturbed early on Christmas morning by the church bells.

"Might as well go to bed," he said to the empty vestry. "Then when I wake up I can open my pressies. But it's going to be a lonely Christmas on my own."

Maximus snuggled down under his duvet. He had managed to find several tissues and a real handkerchief so his bed was really warm and comfortable. Very soon he was asleep and snoring quietly.

Half an hour later there was a strange noise. It sounded as though somebody was trying to get into the vestry through Maximus' special hole. At first the noise didn't wake Maximus but as it got louder he stirred.

Suddenly he was wide awake. There was definitely someone in his vestry. He lay quite still on his bed and listened hard. There were two somebodies – he could hear them whispering. Were they burglars after his Christmas presents? Was he going to be mouseknapped and held to ransom? Perhaps, if he stayed quiet, they would go away again.

After ten minutes he could stand it no longer. They were still there and he had to know what they were doing. He got up very quietly and found the little torch he kept under the bed. He turned it on and shone the beam round the vestry.

There on the carpet by the vicar's desk, holding their paws in front of their eyes to shield them from the light, were two strange mice. They looked very cold and very wet and very tired.

"And just what do you think you are doing?" asked Maximus, sounding braver than he felt. "This is my vestry – you are tresmousing!"

"We're looking for somewhere to stay," said one of the mice. "You see my wife is going to have mouselings very soon. We are mouse holeless and it's freezing outside. Please, please may we stay?"

Maximus scratched his head with his paw. They looked so unhappy that he couldn't throw them out.

"Yes, er ... of course. I expect you're hungry," he went on, "let's see what I can find."

He looked at his Christmas lunch of carol sheet pasta with candlewax sauce. Perhaps that would cheer them up. He soon warmed it and gave it to the visitors. He made some stinging nettle tea and sat with them as they all warmed their paws round the mugs. Maximus put most of his duvet gently round the lady mouse's shoulders and she stopped shivering.

"My name's Joe and my wife's name is Maria.

The house we were living in isn't safe any more. The humans have bought a very unfriendly cat. We've been desperately searching for somewhere to have our first mouselings."

"It is so kind of you, er ... Mr ... um?" said Maria.

"Maximus," said Maximus. "I'm the mousekeeper in this church. I sort of keep an eye on things for the vicar."

"Mr Maximus, it really is very good of you to let us stay."

Maximus found some more warm things for Jo and Maria and they all settled down to sleep. It was quite late on Christmas morning before Maximus woke up again. He yawned and stretched his paws and started to think about what had happened in the night. Then he heard a funny little noise. It was the sort of tiny squeaking noise that Paula's mouselings sometimes made – but they were on holiday!

Maximus jumped out of bed and scampered over to the vicar's desk. There, in an open drawer, was a very proud looking Joe, a tired but happy Maria, and six tiny baby mouselings.

"Maximus, meet your honorary grandchildren," said Jo with a big smile.

Maximus was squeakless. It was just amazing to see the tiny mouselings all nestling up to their mother. Their eyes were shut and they wore very little fur. Maximus' duvet was tucked around them and they seemed warm and happy.

"Well," said Maximus, "I just don't know what to say. It's quite a surprise to wake up to find six new mouselings in my vestry. Congratulations. Have you thought of any names yet?"

"There are two boys and four girls," said Joe. "We thought, if you didn't mind, we would call the older boy Maximus, after you, and the younger one Thomas. The girls will be named after our mothers, Annette and Sophie, and after the children's great grandparents, Eleanor and Patricia."

"I should be very honoured," said Maximus.

. . .

"I hope you weren't too lonely without us," said Paula, when the family came home on Boxing Day.

"Yes, we thought about you being on your own," said Patrick.

"I wasn't on my own," said Maximus. "I had a wonderful Christmas. You see, I had some rather unexpected visitors and they had babies and I'm an honorary grandad."

Maximus told Patrick and Paula the whole story of how Joe and Maria had arrived and how their babies had been born in the vestry, as they didn't have a home of their own.

"It's very strange because that's not really the end," said Maximus. "Just after they had gone to look for a home of their own I went into the church. Lying on the floor under the choir stalls was a carol sheet. I was just about to eat it when some words caught my eye. They were these. They were so nice I learnt them.

Away in a manger, no crib for a bed,
The little Lord Jesus laid down his sweet head.
The stars in the bright sky looked down where he lay,
The little Lord Jesus asleep in the hay.

It sort of reminded me of what happened on Christmas Day in my vestry."

Final Comment: Lots of things happen at Christmas. The most important is to remember the birth of Jesus.

Prayer
Loving Father,
You gave us Jesus at Christmas time. Help us to know him, to love him and to serve him, every day in the year.

Hymn
116   There's a star in the east
120   As I went riding by
75   I saw the man from Galilee
23   Jesus good above all other
24   Go tell it on the mountain
27   There's a child in the street
      or Christmas carols

22　SHARE IS PART OF HARVEST

Theme: Harvest

Aim: To thank God for all his gifts whilst at the same time remembering other people

Preparation: Large individual letters for HARVEST

Story

If there was one season that Maximus looked forward to more than any other – it was harvest. It was the time in the year when people brought lots of lovely food to church. They played a funny sort of game with him – they put the food in lots of different places. He had to chase all over the church to find what he wanted. Fruit was put on the windowsills, vegetables laid round the pulpit, flowers filled vases to overflowing and often there was a sheaf of corn. There was a newly baked harvest loaf, which had a wonderful whisker twitching smell.

Maximus really looked forward to harvest. It wasn't only the adults who brought him lots of food. There was always a Family Service and the children brought baskets and boxes with even more. Maximus was very grateful to everyone but, even with Patrick and Paula and the mouselings, they could never eat it all.

Maximus always liked the harvest hymns. His favourite was 'All things bright and beautiful', because he was sure that the words 'all creatures great and small' were about him. He didn't know who the great was but the small was definitely him.

Maximus had written his own verse to the hymn. It went like this.

'Each little mouse is grateful,
Just listen to them squeak.
So thank you everybody -
Can we have it every week?'

By the time the Family Service started Maximus, Patrick, Paula and the mouselings had already eaten far more than they should. They had found delicious red apples by the organ, a banana on the pulpit, several ears of corn had now disappeared from the big sheaf and there was even a small piece missing from the special harvest loaf.

Maximus and the others always enjoyed Family Services and were usually hiding somewhere in the church listening and joining in. Harvest festival was a must, and they were all there, including the forty-three mouselings. They sang the hymns, listened to the prayers and Bible readings, and waited for the vicar to speak.

"Harvest is a wonderful time," he said. "It is a time when we come to church and say 'thank you' to God for all the good things he has given us. Some people think that harvest is only about food."

"Well, of course it is," whispered Maximus to Patrick. "That's why I think harvest is best."

"But," went on the vicar, "it is much more than that. At harvest we do say 'thank you' to God but we do it for many reasons. I wonder if one of the children would come out and spell HARVEST for me?"

All the mouselings put their paws in the air but of course the vicar didn't see them.

"Right, Louise, how does it go?" said the vicar.

"H, A, R, V, E, S, T," she said.

"Quite right," said the vicar. "Now, please hold this card."

On the card was a large letter H.

"H stands for our HOMES. We thank God at harvest that we have homes. Homes that are warm and clean and comfortable. Homes where we can be part of a loving family."

The vicar gave cards to other children when they came out and they held them up for everyone to see.

"R stands for RECREATION. That's a big word meaning play and games and holidays and having fun and enjoying yourself. We thank God at harvest that we can do these things.

"V stands for VEGETABLES. We may not always like eating green cabbage but we have lots of vegetables and fruit to enjoy. Look around the church and you will see apples and bananas, carrots and cabbage, and many more. You know, I think our church mice enjoy them too – I've noticed some small bites in some of the fruit."

Maximus and the others looked very embarrassed when the vicar said this.

"We have so much food in this country and we really don't know what it is to be hungry. We thank God at harvest for all the food he gives us.

"E stands for EDUCATION. Louise came out to the front and spelled the word HARVEST for us. She was able to do that because she has been to school and learnt to read. We enjoy many things in our lives because of our education – because we can read and write and understand numbers. At harvest we thank God for our education and for all those who teach us.

"T stands for THANKS. At harvest we come to say a very big 'thank you' to God for all the wonderful things that he gives us – our homes, our recreation, our food and our education."

The mouselings started chattering. Paula asked them to be quiet.

"But Mum," said Posie, "the vicar can't spell. He's missed out two letters."

"Sh, ... listen," said Paula, "perhaps he hasn't finished."

"So that's what our letters stand for," the vicar continued. "But H, R, V, E, T don't spell harvest.

119

There are two letters missing. They are special letters. A stands for ALL and S stands for SHARE.

"At harvest we shouldn't just think of ourselves. We should think of ALL people everywhere. We should think of those who have no homes, who cannot play because they are ill, of those who do not ever have enough to eat and of those who have no schools to go to. It is those with whom we should SHARE our harvest.

"As you know, your gifts of food and fruit will be shared with people nearby. Your gifts of money will be used to help those in other countries that do not have a good harvest. As we thank God at harvest for what we have, so we pray for those who have very little."

"There's more to harvest than I ever thought," said Maximus to Patrick after the service. "I must remember those letters."

Final Comment: Harvest is a happy time – made even happier when we share it.

Prayer
Loving Father,
You give us so much – our food, our homes, our schools, our play and the love of those who care for us. Help us to remember that many people are hungry or homeless, have no schools or play. Help us to show them your love by caring for them. Amen

Hymn

133	Give thanks for the sun
138	Now we sing a harvest song
3	All things bright and beautiful
4	Autumn days when the grass is jewelled
7	All creatures of our God and King
8	Let us with a gladsome mind
12	Who put the colours in the rainbow?

23 THERE'S NOTHING ALIVE IN THERE

Theme: Easter

Aim: To show that Jesus came back to life again on Easter Day

Preparation: Picture of a butterfly and chrysalis

Story

It was a perfect autumn day. Maximus and Patrick were enjoying the sunshine as they sat chatting on a stone in the churchyard. Flying just above them were several butterflies, their brightly coloured wings catching the sun.

Suddenly Maximus started to wriggle around and then he tried to scratch himself.

"Got an itch, Maximus?" asked Patrick laughing.

"There's something in my fur on my back," said Maximus. "I can't quite reach it." And he squirmed about again.

"It's a caterpillar," said Patrick, "a little green caterpillar. Poor thing must think it's in the jungle in your fur!"

Patrick gently took the caterpillar from Maximus' fur and put it down on the stone. The mice laughed as it hunched its back and crawled away. Soon it was lost in the grass.

"Amazing things caterpillars and butterflies," said Patrick. "I mean, you and I grew inside our mothers and then we were born in a warm nest. But with butterflies it's different."

"Look," said Maximus. He was pointing at a bush that grew by the churchyard wall. "I've just seen some butterflies land on that. I wonder what they're doing?"

"Wait till they've gone and we'll have a look."

A few moments later the butterflies flew off. The two mice went closer to the bush. It was full of furry caterpillars – lots and lots of them, all chewing the leaves. As well as the caterpillars there were eggs, laid by the butterflies, hanging down from some of the smaller stems of the bush. As they watched, one of the eggs opened, and a tiny caterpillar wriggled out.

"It's amazing – really amazing," said Patrick.

"But what happens now?" asked Maximus. "I mean, it'll be winter soon. Won't the caterpillars just die?"

"I don't think so. For the next few weeks they will eat as many leaves as they can. They'll grow much bigger and then they turn into pupae."

"Into what?" asked Maximus.

"Pupae. It's a bit like you snuggling down under your duvet so no one knows there is a mouse under it. The caterpillar lives inside this sort of sleeping bag for weeks. Another name for pupae is chrysalis."

"And it stays there all through the winter?"

"Yes, some pupae will do that. Anyway it's time I went home. Paula's cooking a couple of pages of organ music for supper. She says organic food is better for you."

The days grew shorter and the nights longer. The weather turned cold and Maximus and Patrick didn't go out into the churchyard very often.

One day, as he wandered about, Maximus saw a strange thing hanging from one of the dried flower stems in the vestry. It was brown and looked a bit like a tiny sock. It seemed to be very dead and uninteresting. He was just about to pull it off the stem when Patrick came in.

"Don't do that," said his friend. "That's what we were talking about weeks ago. It's a pupae or chrysalis. There's a butterfly waiting to come out when the weather's better."

"What a load of rubbish," said Maximus. "Pull the other paw! That's dead. There's nothing alive in there."

"Well, if you don't believe me then at least leave it and watch what happens."

The time went on. The days began to grow longer and lighter again. Maximus kept an eye on the chrysalis but nothing much seemed to happen.

"It's dead," he said to Patrick just before Easter.

"Nothing's going to happen."

On Easter Day the mice went to the Family Service as usual.

There were lots of people singing the hymns about Jesus coming back to life again.

"A very happy Easter to you all," said the vicar.

"And to you too," squeaked the mouselings politely.

"Today is a wonderful day," continued the vicar, "it's the day that Jesus was seen alive again by some of his friends. I wonder how they felt? They knew he had died on the day we call Good Friday. They knew he had been buried in a grave. They must have been terribly sad and unhappy, thinking they would never see him again. Of course not everyone believed that he was alive again. One of Jesus' friends, called Thomas, said 'I won't believe it until I see Jesus myself.' But very soon after that he did see Jesus and he did believe it."

After the service Maximus invited Patrick, Paula and the mouselings back to the vestry.

"I've got a surprise for you," he told the mouselings. The mouselings followed Maximus into the vestry and he gave each of them a tiny chocolate Easter egg.

"Maximus," said Patrick, "I've got a surprise for you too. Look over there." Patrick pointed to the windowsill.

There, in the warm sun, was the most beautiful butterfly. Maximus rushed over to where the chrysalis had been hanging. It was cracked and empty. What had seemed dead had come alive again.

"That is just amazing," said Maximus. "Happy Easter everyone!"

Final Comment: Easter is a happy time because Jesus came back to life again.

Prayer
Heavenly Father,
Thank you that Easter Day follows Good Friday –
that Jesus came back to life again. Help us to live as
those who love a living saviour – Jesus Christ. Amen

Hymn
22   I danced in the morning
128   Trotting, trotting through Jerusalem
129   Jesus in the garden
130   All in an Easter Garden
131   Now the green blade rises from the buried grain

Some other useful school resources...

Aunt Emily's African Animals
Stories and activity ideas for teachers of infants

Brian Ogden
Short animal stories in an African setting for
reading aloud to children. Each one is
followed by a discussion point, a prayer, a
reference to a suitable Bible story and some
activity ideas. An excellent resource for infant
assemblies or class use. Large illustrations
photocopiable.

ISBN 1 85999 182 3
£6.99

Maximus Mouse's Christmas Card and other Christmas plays

Brian Ogden, Marjory Francis, Daphne
Kitching, Angela Weir
A practical resource for busy teachers
looking for fresh Christmas play ideas. This
book is a collection of six plays on Christmas
themes for use with junior age children. All
songs are set to well-known tunes.
Photocopiable resource.

ISBN 1 85999 333 8
£7.99

Everyone Matters: *outlines for junior assemblies*

Tricia Williams (editor)
Outlines for lively and interesting assemblies
suitable for Key Stage 2 pupils, using a variety
of presentation methods. Over 40 outlines in
sections on: Living with Others, God and Me,
Meet Jesus, You're Special. Each outline has
been tried and tested by the contributors.

'*... a wealth of ideas: Highly recommended.*
Association of Christian Teachers

Interactive Assemblies: using drama and puppets

Diane Walker and Jon Webster
Assembly outlines for primary schools which
involve the students in simple drama or
puppetry. Each play is adapted from a Bible
story and is designed for an adult to read the
part of narrator, with simple text for the
children to say in groups. There are teachers'
notes on using puppets in school and
instructions for simple puppets to make in
the classroom. Photocopiable material.

'*The effect is stunning. fast-moving, enthusiastic,
lively...yet...children get the point.*' Together with Children

ISBN 1 85999 253 6
£7.99

'*... a wealth of ideas: Highly recommended.* Association of
Christian Teachers

ISBN 1 85999 040 1
£6.99

Ready-made Assemblies about Famous People

Tony Dobinson
24 assembly outlines for use with Key Stage 2
and 3 pupils. Each assembly is based on the
true life story of a famous Christian including
Jonathan Edwards, Martin Luther King, CS
Lewis, Terry Waite and Mother Teresa. The
assemblies are in five subject groups: creation
and identity; freedom; justice; hope and
forgiveness. Contains invaluable subject-link
index.

All the material you need to prepare an attention-grabbing,
challenging assembly with the minimum of fuss and time.

ISBN 1 85999 300 1
£6.99